ENDORSEMENT

The Creation Dialogues is an excellent defense of the biblical view of origins by creation *ex-nihilo* showing that the so-called theistic evolution view is both unbiblical and unscientific. Both the scriptural and the scientific evidence is effectively and persuasively presented and well documented. Mitchell shows that the attempts by the U.S. government using tax dollars to sell theistic evolution to the public is illegal, wrong-headed, and neither biblical nor scientific. A rewarding read that will benefit both the uninformed as well as the seasoned Christian.

—**Jerry Bergman**, Ph.D.

WinePressPublishing
Your Book, Defined. Since 1991.

WinePress Publishing (PO Box 428, Enumclaw, WA 98022) functions only as book publisher. As such, the ultimate design, content, editorial accuracy, and views expressed or implied in this work are those of the author.

ISBN 13: 978-1-4141-1800-0
ISBN 10: 1-4141-1800-7
Library of Congress Catalog Card Number: 2010905557

CONTENTS

ACKNOWLEDGMENTS

I WOULD LIKE to especially thank Mr. Jim Blunck for introducing me to creation science and the biblical worldview back when I was lost in the foolishness of evolution. Thanks to the Institute for Creation Research, Answers in Genesis, and the Center for Scientific Creation for providing the information I desired when my thirst for creationist materials became nearly insatiable. Dr. Jim Devine provided the encouragement I needed in 2004 when I considered developing my passion for creation science into a formal ministry, and I am gratefully indebted to him for that.

Thanks to Dr. Jerry Bergman as well as the editorial staff at WinePress Publishing for providing numerous suggestions for improving the original manuscript. My sincere appreciation goes to Mr. Paul Abramson for guiding me to a formalized understanding of the evolution vs. creation controversy through my master's degree in Biblical Creation Apologetics. Many thanks to my wife (and true helpmate), Bonnie, for being there by my side as we studied, observed, and learned together the information that is the subject matter of this book. And, last and certainly not least, thanks to our Lord and Savior Jesus Christ for His creation and for His redemptive sacrifice on the cross!

Illustration Credits

All of the illustration images are by the author except for the following:

Illustration 7: Bradley W. Anderson, from *In the Beginning* by Dr. Walt Brown*
Illustration 15: NASA
Illustration 19: G. Elliott Smith, *Illustrated London News*, 24 June 1922, p.944, from *In the Beginning* by Dr. Walt Brown*
Illustration 21: NASA
Illustration 65: NASA

---

*Used by permission

INTRODUCTION

I FIRST LEARNED the details of the American Association for the Advancement of Science (AAAS) position regarding evolution and Christianity when I was asked to provide the biblical creationist viewpoint for an origins study class at a Christian university. The course text for the class was a book entitled *The Evolution Dialogues—Science, Christianity, and the Quest for Understanding* by Catherine Baker and James B. Miller. The book was sponsored and published by the AAAS.

I remember that I had hoped, since the class was designed as an investigation of the various origins belief systems currently held in the culture, that the course text would present a balanced viewpoint.

Once I got a copy of the book and read in the preface the names and affiliations of the editorial advisory committee and then the names of the external reviewers, I knew that my expectations would be dashed. The advisory committee consisted *only* of people from the most liberal denominations of American Christianity, and the external reviewers were all well-known proselytizers for the evolutionary worldview. It was clear that the AAAS position in the book was to attempt to convince Christians that there is no doubt about the fact of biological macroevolution and, therefore, evolution could and should be accepted as compatible with the Christian faith.

Since 1984 when I accepted Christ and began my research into the evolution versus creation controversy, I have found that there is literally no compatibility between the Bible and the Darwinian explanations. As each year has gone by, I have seen more and more indications of the total incompatibility of the two opposite worldviews. Attempting to mix evolution with the plain reading of the Bible is like trying to mix oil with water.

A complete reading of *The Evolution Dialogues* confirmed that the purpose of the book was and is (in the vernacular) to convince the chickens that they can safely open the door of their coop to the foxes.

This book, *The Creation Dialogues—A Response to the Position of American Association for the Advancement of Science on Evolution, Christianity, and the Bible* is a direct result of my reading of The *Evolution Dialogues* and is an attempt to not only critique the contents of the book, but also to refute its premise and AAAS that evolution and Christianity are compatible.

The organization of this book follows the same chapter titles and format as in *The Evolution Dialogues* so that those so inclined can move between the two books chapter by chapter and point by point. However, the reader will find that, unlike *The Evolution Dialogues*, this book will not exhibit such a strong reliance on the words of other so-called experts. There will be a need for some of that, but my greater emphasis will be on what I personally have learned and experienced in my creation science and biblical research over the past 26 years.

In addition, also unlike *The Evolution Dialogues*, this book will place an emphasis on the Creator's Word to mankind. As a result, I trust that the reader will be able to understand the consistency of my presuppositions and the comfort that I have with them. I pray too that because of the content of this book, each reader will be able to develop an awareness of his or her own presuppositions and then use that knowledge to assess if those presuppositions are consistent with his or her conscience.

The Christianity of the Bible is not an accumulation of human traditions and conventions. The Bible (both Old and New Testaments) is the revelation of God's truth for the benefit of all who are open to what it has to say. In 2 Timothy 3:16 we read, "All Scripture is God-breathed and is useful for teaching, rebuking, correcting and training in righteousness, so that the man of God may be thoroughly equipped for every good work." Also in the Bible (e.g. Titus 1:2 and Hebrews 6:18) we are told that God cannot lie; it is against His nature to lie. In 1984, I chose to accept by faith the words of those verses, and the amazing result is that, along the way since then, God has blessed me with an understanding of the consistency between His Special Revelation (the Bible) and His General Revelation (the Creation). Perhaps this book will play a small part in developing a similar understanding in some others.

PROLOGUE

IN *THE EVOLUTION Dialogues*, the prologue, the epilogue, and each of the eight chapters are all prefaced by an ongoing hypothetical story of a Christian girl by the name of Angela Rawlett who leaves the farm to attend college to become a veterinarian. Angela's story is one of how her academic and theological advisors help her move from a mental and spiritual position of distaste for evolutionary philosophy to one of total acceptance. Since I too was once a college student in a similar situation, I will use my actual experiences to comment on each of these prefaces and the worldview the advisors attempt to market.

Angela's Story—Prologue

In the prologue, Angela is introduced to college biology lab and macro evolutionary philosophy. Three evolutionary interpretations are stated as facts without any attempt to substantiate them. When I was in college, I too was bombarded by numerous similar "facts" that I was expected to memorize and then verify by experimentation or just accept. While I was studying to be a physicist, I was enrolled in required courses, which subjected me on a continuing basis to an overriding mystique of Darwinian evolution. After two years, I decided that physics was too esoteric for my tastes and I transferred to the School of Engineering where the evolutionary philosophy for the most part disappeared. However, I found that I was deeply influenced for the rest of my life by that time of evolutionary dogma.

I cannot blame the university for all of this because I got no help on the subject of origins from my church back home, and I was personally very open to the concepts of evolution as presented in my high school biology, chemistry, and physics classes. At my high school, the tradition held that each year we'd sign the yearbooks of friends and acquaintances and add pithy comments for posterity. I was honored that my chemistry teacher signed his name and next to his comment he wrote, "Big Bang or Steady State—that is the question." I took this to mean he felt I held sufficient promise to be able to decide the correct theory for the natural condition of the universe once I completed my education.

Nevertheless in 1984, some 17 years after I graduated from college, I was very angry. I don't know if I was angrier at the church or at the educators, but I do know that I felt I had been lied to for decades regarding origins truth.

PRESUPPOSITIONS

I was so angry because I had previously believed that the facts of evolution were, without any doubt, scientifically proven. I believed this because the academia and science authorities I knew and read had told me so. When I learned instead that these so-called "facts" were merely interpretations determined by certain presuppositions, it became clear to me that I had been led astray. There is nothing wrong with presuppositions driving interpretations; everyone uses them as the foundation for their worldview. However, a presupposition driving an interpretation is not the same as a fact.

The Evolution Dialogues was written with a certain set of presuppositions, and I am writing *The Creation Dialogues* with an entirely different set. Both sets of presuppositions cannot be true, and secondly, although the AAAS and I have exactly the same evidences to study regarding origins issues, we will interpret the evidences differently and come to totally different conclusions.

Triceratops Skull at Carnegie Museum

This book will be in part an attempt to assist the serious reader to understand such concepts as *science, religion, presuppositions, interpretations, evidence, facts, faith,* and *truth,* especially with respect to the questions of origins.

I mentioned earlier that Angela had been introduced to some evolutionary interpretations in her first biology lab. One of these was that "whales descend from a line of hoofed land mammals that returned to the sea" (Page 11). Although stated as a fact, it is an interpretation of evidence based on evolutionary philosophical presuppositions.

Even though my formal training and my career are in the engineering field, since I was a young boy I have always been interested in paleontology. My creation science research has focused in large part on paleontology topics because of this life-long interest. My focus is also in this area because evolutionists use the fossil record as their first argument for evolution when dealing with the media and the general public. Of course, evolutionists believe that the fossil record is a strong evidence for evolution, but in reality the fossil record is one of the most powerful scientific evidences against evolution. Over the decades, my emphasis on paleontology and the fossil record has allowed me to see clearly the presuppositions of evolutionary paleontology, and I will explain them to you shortly.

The scientific method does not allow us to determine the details of the creation of the universe because the creation cannot be repeated in a laboratory or elsewhere. It was a unique historical happening and we have no way to use our senses to develop experiments that might falsify any all-encompassing hypothesis we might dream up. For this reason, neither evolution nor creation can be strictly scientific. However, models can be developed based on presuppositions, and then various theories can be constructed based on those models.

One tremendous advantage that biblical creationists have over evolutionists is that we *do* have an eyewitness to the creation who has provided us with a historical account of what happened. "In the beginning God created the heavens and the earth" (Genesis 1:1). All God-rejecting macro evolutionary theories must be extracted from the minds of men since there is no other reasonable historical record of the beginning outside of the Bible.

The position of *The Evolution Dialogues* and AAAS is that their presuppositions are scientific and that the presuppositions of those who rely on the Bible are religious. This is not my position or the position of many creation scientists and millions of Biblical Christians worldwide who accept the Bible as it is written and who reject the false religion of evolution. As the dialogue of this book develops, I trust the reader will be able to see how we have come to our beliefs that are in total opposition to the AAAS beliefs.

The presuppositions of evolutionary paleontology are:

1. There is no God or God is irrelevant.
2. Everything came from nothing.
3. All lifeforms evolved from common ancestors over billions of years.
4. Homology (the study of similar characteristics) alone proves the evolution of all extinct and living lifeforms.

The earlier whale statement was an interpretation based on these presuppositions. It is not a fact because no one has ever seen hoofed animals returning to the sea to evolve into anything else. The only evidence that evolutionists or creationists have is living hoofed animals, living whales, fossilized bones of hoofed animals, and fossilized bones of whales. All of the animals living or fossilized are completely functional with no indication of hooves changing into flippers or nostrils moving from one place to another. The statement is clearly an unscientific interpretation based on evolutionary presuppositional faith. It is not a fact and it is, at the least, very misleading for evolutionists to make such statements.

Do creationists have presuppositions? Of course they do. Here are the presuppositions normally in place for biblical creationist paleontology:

1. In the beginning God created everything.
2. The Bible is God's true word to mankind.
3. God created in six ordinary days only thousands of years ago.
4. A worldwide Flood destroyed all land animals and humans, except for those on Noah's Ark some 4500 years ago.

It is my experience as a born again Christian that by using creationist presuppositions I can achieve a completely satisfactory consistency between God's Special Revelation (The Bible) and

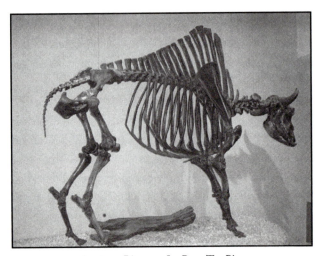

Antique Bison at La Brea Tar Pits

his General Revelation (The Creation). Prior to 1984, when I was attempting to be a theistic or deistic evolutionist, it was impossible to achieve any consistency between the Bible and Darwinian macro evolutionary theories. My situation was as described in Colossians 2:8, which reads, "See to it that no one takes you captive through hollow and deceptive philosophy, which depends on human tradition and the basic principles of this world rather than on Christ." I had indeed been taken captive by the hollow and deceptive philosophy of evolution.

THE VOCAL MINORITY:

The authors of *The Evolution Dialogues* write in their prologue: "What accounts for the *assumption* held by a *vocal minority* of the Christian population that evolutionary theory is a *threat* to their religious beliefs?" [Emphasis mine.] This question is very telling and shines a spotlight on the crux of the matter. Among other things, this statement explains that a primary purpose of the book is to counteract the position of the church minority who are Biblical Christians, that is, those who believe the Bible is authoritative, accurate, and inerrant. I will next dissect this statement on several points by looking at the words "assumption," "vocal minority," and "threat."

1. "Assumption." Biblical creationists are not *assuming* anything. We have over 200 years of recorded history to study that clearly shows that the early and present proponents of evolution and millions of years did not have, and do not have, any interest in preserving the Bible as the source for the triune God's accurate, inerrant, and authoritative Word. Those Christians who actually read their Bibles daily know that there is no harmony between evolutionary theories and the sacred Scriptures. The only way to read evolution and millions of years into the Bible is to force those ideas in there using the process of *eisegesis*, the process of reading into the text what they think is there. Instead, the proper process of biblical interpretation, *exegesis*, extracts meaning from what is already written. Millions of years and evolution simply are not already written in the sacred text. Liberal churches have decades of experience at eisegesis and so would have no problem with hollow and deceptive philosophies. Compromising of God's Word by many in the Church has assisted in the secular world's continuing efforts at marginalizing the Bible and the Christian faith.

    In the last 50 years we have watched a perfect correlation between evolutionary philosophical acceptance in the Church and the nearly total extinction of the Christian Church in Europe. The quick demise of Christianity in Great Britain since World War II has been particularly striking. And in the United States, we are currently witnessing the same process as proponents of secular humanism (like AAAS) work to erode the Christian foundations that once were strongly evident in America. Along with this epidemic of compromise has come a precipitous drop in morals, not only in American society as a whole, but in the Church itself.

2. "Vocal Minority." Yes, biblical creationists are definitely a minority in the Christian body. But, Truth is not determined by a show of hands. The Bible calls for the unity of the Christian and his congregation (e.g. see 1 Corinthians), but there can be no unity without Truth. For every mention of *unity* in the Bible, 18 times *truth* is mentioned. It is clear that we are not to compromise the truth out of our faith for the sake of unity.

    Let me interject another interesting word-count exercise: *Create, Creator, creation,* and *creatures* are mentioned in the Bible 216 times. *Evolution* or any concept that could reasonably be construed as meaning *evolution* is never mentioned! In addition, the genealogies of the Bible limit the age of the creation to 8,000 years or less.

3. "Threat." Biblical creationists do not necessarily believe that evolutionary theories are a threat to their personal beliefs. What they want to emphasize (especially to Christians) is that these theories are a threat to Truth. If the evolutionary theories are true then Christianity cannot be true because the theories are not intrinsically congruous with the Bible on which the Christian faith is based.

Jesus Christ and all the writers of the New Testament believed that Genesis chapters 1 through 11 were historical narratives. If the creation and the worldwide Flood as described in Genesis and elsewhere in the Bible are myths or allegories, then that indicates that Christ was either a liar or ignorant of His creation.

Those Christian denominations that do not have any trouble reconciling evolutionary biology with their faith do so because they have rejected the Word of God. They may or may not reject Christ as their Redeemer, but if they do not reject Him they have no logical reason to accept Him as Redeemer. Rejecting the Fall and the curse negates understanding why Christ needed to come to earth to redeem us. If evolution and millions of years are true, then it cannot be true that death was the result of man's sin since death, suffering, and disease occurred for millions of years before Adam came on the scene. Remember that the Bible clearly teaches that "The wages of sin is death" and that Adam and Eve were sent out of the Garden of Eden and sentenced to death because of their original sin. Sure, many Christians can reconcile evolution with their traditions, but biblical creationists point out that God's Word is what counts, not the traditions of men.

And, the argument goes both ways. AAAS must assume that the Bible is a threat to their religious beliefs or they wouldn't commission the book *The Evolution Dialogues* to try to talk Christians out of believing the inerrancy, authority, and accuracy of the Bible. Evolutionists must indeed feel threatened because they have people such as Eugenie Scott running around the country attempting to silence anyone in public education who might introduce the slightest doubt about the truth of evolutionary theories.

After receiving the light of biblical creation truth in 1984, I was able to begin the process of shedding the baggage of my university evolutionary indoctrination and accept Christ as my Lord and Savior. Now, some 26 years later, I have come to the point where I can see that my purpose on earth is to attempt to help others see the fallacy of evolution in the light of the truth of God's Word. My hope is that my influence might assist some to open their hearts to the Truth and, as I did, allow the Creator to come in. I know that I cannot personally lead anyone to Christ, but perhaps can facilitate the Holy Spirit to enter the lives of a few of the elect. And no matter my success at that task, I trust that my ministry will continue to encourage other Christians to believe the Bible from the very first verse.

Beauty and Design are Obvious in Lifeforms

In 1 Peter 3:15 we read, "Sanctify the Lord God in your hearts; and be ready always to give an answer to every man that asks you a reason of the hope that is in you with meekness and fear." In Greek, the word "answer" is *apologia* from which we get the word "apologetics." An apologetic in this context, then, is the logical defense of the Christian faith against the attacks of its adversaries.

My ministry as a creation science speaker, researcher, and author means that my beliefs are often attacked. The people who most often attack the beliefs of young earth biblical creationists are compromised Christians and brazen atheists. In Romans 1:20-22 we read, "For since the creation of the world God's invisible qualities—his eternal power and divine nature—have been clearly seen, being understood from what has been made, so that men are without excuse. For although they knew God, they neither glorified him as God nor gave thanks to him, but their thinking became futile and their foolish hearts were darkened. Although they claimed to be wise, they became fools."

With this Scripture as a primary reference, I have developed separate apologetics for people in the two groups as follows:

Apologetic for Christians

People can and do believe anything. However, you need to understand that evolution (change from one kind to another kind) and millions of years are not anywhere to be found in God's Word. Evolution and millions of years are presuppositional concepts based directly on deism and atheism. These are God-rejecting philosophies (not science) that were formalized in the 18th and 19th centuries, and that thoroughly permeate our present-day culture due to decades of media and academia indoctrination (a.k.a. secular humanism).

Why you as a Christian would want to distort the truth of God's Word and accept atheistic and deistic philosophy into your faith is a question you alone must reconcile in your own mind. Have you not noticed the significance of the fact that so many of your arguments against Biblical Christianity are based on the ever-changing speculations of secular science?

My recommendation is that you carefully analyze your presuppositions to see if you really want to hold to them. A Christian faith that accepts atheistic and deistic presuppositions is not consistent, but rather is just the opposite—totally inconsistent. Do not succumb to futile thinking and a foolish heart.

Apologetic for Atheists

The second group consists of people who usually call themselves Atheists. They believe there is no God and the universe somehow came about by accident. This position does not allow for logic since, if we are an accident, there is no reason to believe that we would even be able to think, let alone communicate with each other. Nevertheless, I have an apologetic (defense) for this group, which is as follows:

People can and do believe anything. If you want to reject God, He will allow you to do so. But, before you leave this life, be sure you analyze your presuppositions very carefully. If, after completing this careful analysis of your presuppositions, you are still comfortable with them, realize you have chosen a path of total hopelessness.

Also, consider why you would want to attack the Biblical Christian worldview. If the biblical worldview is wrong and the atheistic view true, why would you care to discourage those who have a great hope? What good comes from that? Nothing comes from that except evil! You tell me you are able to have "evolved" morals that are able to direct you to good and not evil. So why not just leave Biblical Christians alone? In the end we will all just be worm food according to your worldview. What does it all matter to you what Christians believe?

On the other hand, if our worldview as revealed by God's Word is true and you are wrong, you will spend eternity in Hell and we will spend eternity in Heaven with God.

Yes, consider your presuppositions carefully! Don't succumb to futile thinking and a foolish heart. There is still a little time left for you to accept Christ's gracious and most generous offer. (Read John 3:16-20).

SCIENCE & RELIGION

A big falsity that evolutionists promote about biblical creationists is that they are anti-science. In *The Evolution Dialogues* (p. 14) is written, "Angela's story reflects how each of us comes to understand our world in community with others. It is a model for how individuals might use dialogue to find an accord between science and religion." Well, I could write the exact same thing in my book *The Creation Dialogues* with the only difference being "J.D.'s story."

The Evolution Dialogues' inference that biblical creationists cannot find an accord between science and Christianity is total nonsense! I can speak for nearly all creationists when I say we tend to find a consistent and nearly perfect accord between true science and the biblical account. However, we are unable to find accord between the religion of naturalism (which is based on evolutionary theories) and our faith in God's Word. Again, just because the proponents of evolution define evolution as science does not make it so. We would say that evolution is science falsely so called. All macro-evolutionary theories are based on philosophy and the anti-God presuppositions mentioned earlier. They are not based on any sort of normal experimental science. A good example of the development of this philosophy will be evident when we look into the lives of Charles Lyell and George Young later in this book.

HYSTERIA

On page 15 of *The Evolution Dialogues* we read, "This volume is one effort by AAAS to help engage the latter group [liberal Christians], because very much *is* at stake. We are talking about the quality of public science education and the scientists who come out of that enterprise, the integrity of science as an independent enterprise, and the constitutional division between church and state."

This sort of statement is typical of those written by the Nazis prior to World War II. For example, the Nazis perpetrated a campaign to diminish the value of the lives of certain types of people. Anyone who didn't agree with their way of thinking was also defined as undesirable, and that is what the AAAS is trying to do to creation scientists and Biblical Christians. The only scientists that have any need on a daily basis for evolutionary theory are evolutionary biologists, paleontologists, anthropologists, geologists, etc. All other science (basic or applied) has been done and can continue to be done on a daily basis without any need for evolutionary theories. The hysteria exhibited by the AAAS and others like them can be boiled down to two root causes:

1. People want to reject God, so they look to accept a Godless faith such as naturalism or pantheism, its related cousin.
2. Money.

I'll address the second cause of hysteria first. The people who make their livelihood from evolutionary theories rely almost exclusively on funds from or through academic or governmental organizations. The evolutionist academia has developed an entire body of "knowledge" consisting of many thousands of published papers and books, all based on the so-called truth of macro evolution and millions of years. These folks and their predecessors have devoted their careers to this story and are so deep into it that they see no way out. Anyone who would decide to question the paradigm would not only be ostracized by the evolutionary community that controls academia, but would, in effect, have to throw away their life's work! The pressure on this group of people is enormous to accept and then stay in the faith.

A few years ago I was personally discussing a homology paper I had written with a famous dinosaur paleontologist at a large natural history museum in the United States. I expressed my concern that he and most other secular paleontologists refused to look at the fossil record evidences with an open mind. He said to me, "J.D., don't you know that science is not about truth."

As you may imagine, I was flabbergasted by his response. The word "science" means knowledge and not philosophy. It was not until later that I came to understand what he was attempting to tell me, and that was that evolutionary science is more about money than truth.

This famous paleontologist, who had worked hard for years to achieve his esteemed position in the academic community, believed he had no choice but to stay to the evolutionary lie or else lose his entire life's work and any hope he might have for continuing in his career. I can certainly sympathize with this man and others who are in a similar situation.

Now let me go to the first reason I listed for evolutionist hysteria. If evolution is a fact of science, as AAAS and others in their camp say, why are they so afraid to allow dialogues in the public schools that point out the myriad weaknesses of their theory and the strengths of the alternative paradigm? The reason is clear: The evolutionary paradigm cannot stand on its own. It is so weak that it will fail in the eyes of most reasonable, open-minded thinkers once the biblical alternative is fully revealed in contrast with God-less evolutionary theories. In an open forum, those who cling to the naturalistic faith see their world crashing down around them. They evidently believe that their only recourse is to throw up artificial barriers to any alternative ideas outside of their naturalism concept. And so far the media and the courts have chosen to go along with them.

Finally, if the AAAS and the writers of the *Evolution Dialogues* really wanted a public dialogue, they would welcome all ideas into the origins discussion, not just those that fit their methodological naturalism worldview.

CHAPTER 1
SCIENCE IN DARWIN'S TIME

ANGELA'S STORY

IN ANGELA'S FIRST meeting with her college advisor, she is quoted Theodosius Dobzhansky's words, "Nothing in biology makes sense except in the light of evolution." Angela's advisor then said, "You need this foundation if you really want to understand plants."

These quotes, one historical and one hypothetical, both seem true for those who have wittingly or unwittingly accepted evolutionary presuppositions. Once Angela actually gets into the study of biology, however, all she will find is complex design and functional lifeforms. She will never see any instance of macro evolution in process because it never occurs. If she is to "toe-the-mark" for her instructors and advisors at this college, she will have to learn to accept the macro evolutionary presuppositions totally on faith.

As an engineer with decades of design experience, I know that nothing in nature can design itself. Every design requires information, and the information is in place only due to intelligent sources. As Angela moves through her biology classes, she will have to accept one fairy tale after another to explain how design can result from the random interaction of matter. Yes, "science is based on the study of evidence," but the evidence is interpreted according to the presuppositions. Everyone

Multnomah Falls in the Columbia River Gorge

1

has the same evidence, but since the presuppositions are varied, the interpretations will also be varied.

We could happily end Angela's story at this time by simply having her drop out of this college and enroll at a Christian college that teaches biology with biblical presuppositions. In that case she would be able to learn what she needs for her career as a veterinarian, and in addition, she would not emotionally upset her family and her church members. At the same time, she would not need to accept the atheistic and deistic presuppositions that are foundational to evolution.

The fact is that the college Angela has chosen has decided to indoctrinate their students rather than educate them. Angela's advisor quoted Dobzhansky regarding biology and evolution as at least an important precept if not a fact. That Dobzhansky's statement was a philosophical position is clear from Dobzhansky's own words, such as:

> It would be wrong to say that the biological theory of evolution has gained universal acceptance among biologists or even among geneticists. This is perhaps unlikely to be achieved by any theory which is so extraordinarily rich in philosophic and humanistic implications.[1]

and,

> Evolution is a process which has produced life from non-life, which has brought forth man from animals, and which may conceivably continue doing remarkable things in the future. In giving rise to man, the evolutionary process has, apparently for the first and only time in the history of the cosmos, become conscious of itself.[2]

Dobzhansky is very aware of the philosophic basis for the biological theory of evolution; and his second quote above is a perfect example of an evolutionary faith statement.

On page 19 of *The Evolution Dialogues*, in the body of Angela's story is a photo of the Venus fly trap. One would assume that the authors placed this photo there as an example of the wonders that evolution has created. Creationist explanations for the wonders of living things are ignored.

> The Venus fly trap is a wonder of God's engineering. It has an ingenious method, quite different from other plants, for getting food. This meat-eating plant usually lives in mineral-poor soils. Therefore, it catches its food in order to provide the needed nutrients for survival. When an insect touches the tiny trigger hairs inside the trap, an electric signal is sent to cells on the outside of the trap. This impulse almost instantly causes the outer cells to secrete an acid which breaks down the cell wall. This, in turn, causes cells to expand, closing the trap at high speed. The more the insect fights, the more tightly the trap closes. Six to twelve days later, after the

insect is digested, the plant receives a chemical signal and the trap opens to await its next meal. Why do animals, and even plants, have to fight each other for their very survival? Is this really the creation that God described as "very good"? Actually, it is not. All of creation exhibits fallen, aggressive nature due to the actions of Adam and Eve in the original garden paradise. It is unknown whether the complex mechanisms of survival demonstrated by the Venus fly trap were present but dormant before the Fall, or were designed within the plant for survival after the Fall. Either way, the Venus fly trap is a marvel of purposeful design which gives testimony to the genius behind its creation.[3]

SCIENCE IN DARWIN'S TIME

A period of unprecedented scientific discovery

I have no problem with the historical information in *The Evolution Dialogues* in chapter 1 except for two points. The first is that the authors fail to mention that many of the men who made these scientific discoveries during Darwin's time were creationists. Students of the advancements in science of the 18th and 19th centuries are familiar with men such as Robert Boyle, George Washington Carver, Michael Faraday, John Ambrose Fleming, James Joule, Matthew Maury, Joseph Clerk Maxwell, Gregor Mendel, Samuel F.B. Morse, Isaac Newton, Louis Pasteur, and William Ramsay. These men made great discoveries because they believed the Bible and, therefore, expected to find an orderly and understandable universe.

Carolus Linnaeus devoted his life to classifying plants and animals, and the Linnaean system of classification is still used today. "One of his main goals in systematizing the tremendous varieties of living creatures was to attempt to delineate the original Genesis 'kinds.'"[4]

The second major point of disagreement is *The Evolution Dialogues'* authors' interpretation of the age of the earth.

Rethinking the age of the Earth

Comte de Buffon, James Hutton, and Charles Lyell indeed did propose, assert, conjecture, and theorize that the world was much older than the record of events and lineages as recorded in the Bible. They and others of the 18th and 19th centuries who made these "unbelievable propositions" certainly did *not* have any firm proof for these claims. In fact, today, there is still no scientific proof for these old earth claims.

Radiometric dating methods developed in the 20th century are usually cited by evolutionists as scientific proof for the supposed 4.6 billion year age of the Earth. But radiometric dating and other uniformitarian dating methods are all based on unproven and unprovable assumptions. These assumptions are basically as follows:

1. The amount of parent material is known at the beginning of the time segment.
2. The rate of change (or decay) of the measured process is constant and is the same as the current measured rate.
3. No contamination of the parent or daughter materials has occurred during the time segment.

Scores of these types of uniformitarian estimation methods exist that can be, and have been, used to attempt to determine the earth's age. These methods are all fundamentally flawed because of the inability to scientifically test the assumptions. In addition, the different methods do *not* come up with the same estimated age of the earth. One list compiled by the Institute for Creation Research displays 68 different processes with resulting estimated ages ranging from "too small to measure" to a maximum of "500,000,000" years.[5] All of these processes result in ages that are far less than the secularly accepted 4.6 billion year age of the earth. In fact, two-thirds of these estimates result in an age of a million years or less, and one-third result in an age of 10,000 years or less.

The fact that evolutionists choose to use uniformitarian methods that utilize processes that result in the oldest ages instead of an average or some other combination is an indication of the philosophical foundation for their "science." In reality, there will never be enough time for macro evolutionary changes to occur in lifeforms, but billions of years does make the impossible seem a little more plausible to those open to the evolutionary story.

Let's focus first on Charles Lyell, "the founder of modern geology."

From a study of the life of Charles Lyell (1797-1875) we can learn how he thought and how he came to believe what he thought. His life is also an accurate reflection of many of the so-called scientific giants of his time. Not only was Lyell and others like him driven by distaste for the excesses of the state run Anglican Church, but they also felt they were discovering new hidden truths of Nature with a capital 'N'—truths they felt minimized or obliterated the need for a Creator God. The study of the lives of Charles Lyell, James Hutton, Charles Darwin, Thomas Huxley, and other Bible minimalists is very important for today's Christians. This is because by studying their lives, we can learn that even though they may have at times exhibited competent experimental science, the effect they had on today's world was mostly through the philosophies they developed and promoted and not through their science.

Not everyone understands that so-called "natural history" or "historical science" is really not either history or science. The study of origins cannot be a study of history because the past is unproven and unprovable without historical documentation. Secular science supported by naturalistic evolutionary philosophy has no historical documentation to rely on concerning the origin of the universe, earth, or life on earth. Therefore, nothing can really be definitely known about origins through the sole use of the scientific method.

On the other hand, Christians have God's Word, the only ancient document that provides that history; and since we believe that God would not lie to us, we have good reason to accept His account of the creation as being accurate and factual. With that as a foundational premise we also find the creation itself can be easily correlated with the biblical account.

Charles Lyell was an untiring advocate for uniformitarianism and millions of years. He believed that by presupposing that the present observable geological operations are the key to all past geology, he could forensically reconstruct the past. He rejected any possibility of a major catastrophe in the past, a concept mostly abandoned by today's geologists, who recognize that much of the earth's surface was formed by catastrophic actions not experienced today. It is true that the majority of secular scientists cannot conceive of a worldwide flood, but this is due to their presuppositions not because of the evidence.

It is my opinion that without the influence of Charles Lyell on early 19th century academia and without the acceptance of his uniformitarian ideas by much of the Christian church, it is doubtful that Charles Darwin would have published his *Origin of Species* (1859). Lyell was a friend of Darwin's and (along with Joseph Hooker) was instrumental in talking a reluctant Darwin into publishing his hypothesis regarding evolution by natural selection.

Darwin's earlier book *The Voyage of the Beagle*, which documents Darwin's travels from December of 1831 through October 1836, Darwin dedicated as follows: "To Charles Lyell, Esq. F.R.S. This second edition [1845] is dedicated with grateful pleasure, as an acknowledgement that the chief part of whatever scientific merit this journal and the other works of the author may possess, has been derived from studying the well-known and admirable *Principles of Geology*."

So, without Lyell's influence it is quite clear that Darwin would not have had the "long ages" required to conceive of some sort of macro-evolutionary hypothesis. Charles Lyell wrote numerous letters over his career, many of which were reprinted in a two volume work by his sister-in-law in 1881, some six years after Lyell's death. Titled *Letters and Journals of Sir Charles Lyell*, anyone who reads these volumes of Lyell's writings should be able to see that his lifework in geology was influenced more by his philosophy than by his science.

The layman's common sense and experience tells him that the past determines the present, which is exactly opposite to uniformitarianism, which states that the "present is the key to the past." Yet, it is so easy to accept ridiculous concepts just because they are promoted by an educated authority.

The scriptural geologists of Lyell's time, such as George Young, did not accept those "ridiculous" concepts and strongly objected to them. Unfortunately, much of the Church did and still does accept them.

The life of Rev. George Young, D.D. (1778-1848) is a counterpoint to Charles Lyell. The reason is Young long ago identified and countered the geological philosophies of Lyell. Yes, uniformitarianism has been mostly refuted since the time that Lyell wrote in the 19th century, but the single aspect of geological uniformity still held by today's secular geologists is that which rejects the worldwide Genesis Flood so plainly described in the Bible. In 1838, George Young published his young earth biblical answer to Lyell (and other anti-biblical writers of the time) titled, *Scriptural Geology or an Essay on the High Antiquity Ascribed to the Organic Remains Imbedded in Stratified Rocks*.

George Young was an intelligent, educated scholar who distinguished himself at the University of Edinburgh, especially in mathematics and natural philosophy. Young published 21 books, three on the subject of geology. Young was qualified to consider and counter Lyell's uniformitarianism philosophy as he had extensive geological field experience.

Author Terry Mortenson has written the book *The Great Turning Point* (Master Books, 2004) that provides more extensive biographical information on Young and six other qualified scriptural geologists who were largely ignored by the Church in the 19th century and following. I highly recommend Mortenson's book to anyone interested in the topic of "millions of years" and the influence of this philosophy on the Church.

Today's secular humanist culture and much of the Christian church continues to honor Lyell and his ilk (even though their ideas have been replaced in large part by today's neocatastophism), while unfairly ignoring the work of Young and the other scriptural geologists. Do Christians follow the secularists like sheep to the slaughter? I say no! We should read the writings of Young and Lyell and determine for ourselves what was science, what was philosophy, what is truth, and what is not truth.

In Young's *Scriptural Geology*, he respectfully mentioned Lyell at least a dozen times, so there is no doubt that Young was well aware of Lyell's viewpoint. And Young logically and scientifically countered Lyell's opinions while steadfastly staying to the biblical account, as today's creation scientists attempt to do.

Pondering the succession of life

Uniformitarians use *correlation* to tie together the sedimentary rock layers throughout the world to match their millions of years concept. That is, they correlate sedimentary layers in one part of the world to those in another part of the world, usually through index fossils and/or the mineral makeup of the layers. This concept of correlation is based on uniformitarianism and suffers from numerous problems with matching reality. For example, not all the layers are represented in all areas of the world. There are millions of years worth of layers missing in most locations where the layers are found.

In addition, fossils continue to provide more evidence each year that the Rock Record is not a record of billions of years. This is because the lifeforms found in the fossil record show abrupt appearance, no transitional forms, stasis, and a tendency for expansion of their range of presence in the record with each passing year of fossil discoveries.

Coelacanth Living Fossil at Smithsonian Museum

This range expansion manifests itself in what is often called "topsy-turvy" fossils by creation scientists. The evolutionists have different names for the phenomenon, such as anomalous fossil sequences, and they usually explain away the "improper" fossil sequence with what they call reworking. The examples of reworking are becoming more and more ubiquitous.

Topsy-turvy fossils come in two basic categories. The first includes those fossils that are initially found lower in the fossil record and assumed to be extinct. Later they work their way up in the record (with additional discoveries) so that the presumed locations of time segment boundaries in the column have to be modified or the supposed evolutionary relationships have to be revised. When the assumed extinct organism happens to work its way "up" to the point of living in the here and now, the organism is renamed a "living fossil." There are over 500 identified living fossils extant today. Living fossils strongly deteriorate the credibility of the philosophy behind the so-called Geologic Column and organic macroevolution.

But topsy-turvy fossils are also found expanding from higher locations in the column to lower locations. The overall reality is that there are no indications of evolution in the fossils, and close to identical lifeforms are found throughout the entire extent of the Rock Record with increasing frequency. As this occurs, evolutionary paleontologists are left only with the evolutionary presupposition of homology to support their philosophical worldview, and homology has a very wobbly foundation itself. Homology, the study of structural similarities in lifeforms, is a foundational presupposition of evolutionary paleontology.

This situation of topsy-turvy fossils is exactly what the creation model with its worldwide Flood would predict and always has predicted. Life was formed initially according to its kinds with the ability for limited adaptation built in due to the information in its DNA. From this vantage point, the fossil record is mainly evidence for a universal catastrophic flood.

A few years ago my wife and I participated in a dinosaur dig in the badlands of eastern Montana. What really struck me during this dig was the rapidity at which the terrain in this area was being *eroded away.* Yet the sedimentary layers in which we dug for dinosaur bones and other plant and animal fossils are so-called Cretaceous age. That means they are supposed to be 65 to 100 million years old, according to the evolutionary theory and the uniformitarian Geologic Column. If these layers were laid down over 65 million years ago, it is obvious that they should have all totally eroded away long ago. Remember that the principle of uniformity is supposed to translate the ages of these sediments according to the rates of today.

Badlands near Glendive, Montana

Many Uniformitarians have abandoned the concept of uniformity *except* with regard to its application to a worldwide flood. Catastrophe is accepted more and more by secular geologists, such as with regard to the Missoula Flood.

Finally, think about the concept of *correlation* again. If the present is the key to the past, then we would not expect correlation for geologic processes over long periods of time! For example, today all over the world different geologic processes occur at different rates. In some places, sediments are being laid down, and in other places, they are being eroded away and carried away into the oceans. Today, no sediments can last long without portions of them being severely eroded. In today's observable world, geologic processes are not forming a worldwide geologically correlated record.

If there is indeed correlation today in what is seen in the Rock Record, then that would indicate a *single event,* not millions of events over millions of years. This matches the biblical creationist model of a one-year-long worldwide catastrophic flood not too long ago. Correlation logically makes no sense for millions or billions of years of geologic uniformity! The Geologic Column looks to be quickly crumbling away as a model for long ages.

The Bible says in 2 Peter 3:3-6:

"First of all, you must understand that in the last days scoffers will come, scoffing and following their own evil desires. They will say, 'Where is this coming he promised? Ever since our fathers died, everything goes on as it has since the beginning of creation.' But they deliberately forget that long ago by God's word the heavens existed and the earth was formed out of water and by water. By these waters also the world of that time was deluged and destroyed."

Darwin makes his contribution

Evolutionists often accuse creationists of claiming that species don't change and they were created in the beginning by God as distinct, static species. But that is a straw man argument designed to deflect the focus of scientific inquiry away from the real truth.

It is obvious that species do change through natural and artificial selection (breeding) as Darwin knew. There is definitely variability within species, and no reputable creation scientist denies this. An example is in the many varieties of dogs that have been bred by man over the centuries. In the beginning was a basic dog kind that now manifests itself in many varieties as developed by natural and artificial selection over the thousands of years since the creation. However, after all of these years, all of these species are still dogs. They started out as dogs and have changed over time to be nothing but dogs. This fact tells us that a dog can never be bred to have wings, for example, because the genetic information for wings is not in the dog DNA. Another familiar example is that human children look different from their parents. These children are never exactly the same as their parents but are still obviously humans; and the science of genetics confirms that they will *never* be able to naturally sprout wings no matter how many generations are propagated.

If we look past the straw man arguments of the evolutionists, we find that creation scientists believe that true science confirms that *microevolution* (variability) does indeed occur but that *macroevolution* (change from one kind to another kind) has not and cannot occur because of the limits on the information that God placed in the DNA of each kind in the beginning as described in the book of Genesis. This fact means that our interpretation of reality (our science) indicates that the concept of all of life evolving from a common ancestor over millions of years is a fairy tale. What we see from true science, therefore, matches up to the information provided by God in the Bible. This is what the Christian should expect.

Another interesting fact that continues to be reinforced by ongoing science is that the micro-evolutionary changes that do occur in lifeforms always tend to *reduce* the overall capability of an organism to adapt to future changes in its environment. This micro-evolutionary process is actually *devolution* rather than evolution. This is because the process of change results in a *loss* of information. In fact, there is no known natural method for the introduction of *new information* into any genome. In the case of dogs, what this means is that the poodle dog (as an example) can never be expected to re-evolve back to the original dog kind, which had a much greater capability for adaptation to environmental changes. The poodle dog has lost much of the original genome adaptive capability that was in the original dog kind.

Evolutionists also use spurious arguments (especially to the unwary, such as our school children) such as since there are numerous examples of microevolution in nature, given enough time, macroevolution must eventually occur. But this is not at all true. Think of it this way. Imagine a railroad track that runs across the United States from coast to coast represents time. Now, the evolutionist will often say that if a locomotive representing micro-evolutionary change starts at the west coast and makes even an infinitesimal progress toward moving east, it can eventually make it all the way to the east coast. It is just a matter of enough time. Therefore, macroevolution is proven true by this analogy.

But this visual model is flawed. A reality-representative railroad track analogy would be quite different.

In the model representing reality we would have two locomotives located on the track and sitting at the center of the continent. One locomotive representing microevolution would be headed to the west, and the other representing macroevolution would be headed the opposite direction toward the east. True science shows that the locomotive headed east *never* moves at all and exists only in the imaginations of evolutionists. The east coast bound locomotive could be provided billions upon billions of years but no progress would be seen because macroevolution does not and cannot happen.

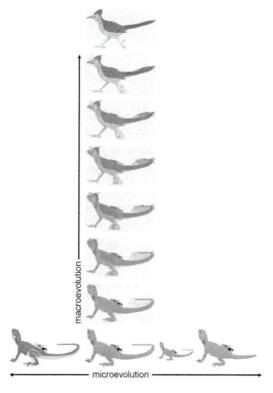

The west coast bound locomotive would show some movement representing micro evolutionary changes, and the changes might occasionally represent organism survival improvement as the genome is constantly deteriorating from its original perfect state. Those changes helpful to the organism could be considered "designed adaptability" to allow the organism a better chance for survival in a more challenging environment. This designed adaptability was provided for by the Creator in the beginning when the original kinds were created. Naturalism is a philosophy (religion really) that rejects God as clearly revealed in the

Macroevolution vs. Microevolution

Bible and in His creation. People who cling to this religion believe by faith that all that exists is nature and that the universe came to be according to some evolutionary fairy tale.

Unfortunately, many Christians have unnecessarily allowed themselves to be influenced by these fairy tales that run counter to their faith and true science. The Bible warns us, "See to it that no one takes you captive through hollow and deceptive philosophy, which depends on human tradition and the basic principles of this world rather than on Christ" (Colossians 2:8).

In today's culture, naturalism is the "basic principle of the world." Don't allow it to take you captive.

In his book *The Origin of Species,* Darwin wrote, "as this process of extermination [or survival of the fittest] has acted on an enormous scale, so must the number of intermediate varieties, which have formerly existed on the earth, be truly enormous. Why then is not every geological formation and every stratum full of such intermediate links? Geology assuredly does not reveal any such finely graduated organic chain; and this, perhaps, is the most obvious and gravest objection which can be urged against my theory. The explanation lies, as I believe, in the extreme imperfection of the geologic record."[6]

In fact, Darwin devoted all of chapter ten to this imperfection of the geologic record. If Darwin were alive today he would, over 150 years later, have to repeat those same concerns. Some estimates are that paleontologists have uncovered and catalogued over a billion fossils in the past 200 years. Yet there are no examples in the fossil record of one animal slowly changing into a different kind of animal. Herbert Spencer's and Darwin's use of the terminology "survival of the fittest" is really a tautology (a needless repetition of an idea in a different phrase). This is because the lifeforms that survive are defined as the fittest, and the fittest are the ones that survive. Evolutionary theories provide no insight regarding which lifeforms or species may or may not exist at any time in the future.

On page 33 of *The Evolution Dialogues,* the authors state, "However, it becomes clear that Mendelian genetics explains much of the pattern of variation that Darwin observed among offspring. It is on this variation that natural selection operates to bring about descent with modification."

Creation scientists would agree that statement explains the process of microevolution that is observed in the living and fossil lifeforms. They would not, however, agree that Gregor Mendel's work or Charles Darwin's observations provide the slightest proof of the evolution of all life from an ancient common ancestor.

FURTHER READING

1. Denton, Michael, *Evolution: A Theory in Crisis,* Adler & Adler, 1986.
2. Gitt, Werner, *In the Beginning Was Information,* Christliche Literatur-Verbeitung e.v., 1997.
3. Lyell, Charles, *Life, Letters and Journal of Sir Charles Lyell in Two Volumes,* John Murray, 1881.
4. Morris, Henry, *Men of Science Men of God,* Master Books, 1988.
5. Morris, Henry & Parker, Gary, *What Is Creation Science?* Master Books, 1987.
6. Mortenson, Terry, *The Great Turning Point,* Master Books, 2004.
7. Sarfati, Jonathan, *Refuting Evolution,* Master Books, 1999.
8. Sunderland, Luther, *Darwin's Enigma,* Master Books, 1988.
9. Young, George, *Scriptural Geology,* Simpkin & Marshall, 1838.

CHAPTER 2
CHRISTIANITY IN DARWIN'S TIME

ANGELA'S STORY

AT THE BEGINNING of chapter 2, Angela meets with a man named Phil in the campus ministry offices. And here begins in earnest *The Evolution Dialogues'* subtle attack on Biblical Christianity and the Bible.

Angela tells Phil that she assumed that, if she went to a representative of the campus ministries, she would receive biblically based advice similar to what she would receive from the Christians she knew and trusted back home. It turns out this was a very erroneous assumption on her part.

Most of the original American colleges (e.g. Yale and Harvard) were established as Christian institutions. Today these same colleges and universities are totally secular. The decline of these institutions from reliance on God's Word to a reliance on the words of men followed almost simultaneously with the acceptance of evolution and millions of years by many compromising liberals and academics in the Church. Along with this attack on the literal interpretation of the Bible came the so-called "higher criticism" that has questioned all aspects of the Gospel message. Today it is not an exaggeration to describe a high percentage of American institutions of higher learning as bastions of Satan.

Satan has always used the same technique to lead people on the wrong path away from their Creator and Redeemer. In Genesis 3:1 we read, "Now the serpent was more crafty than any of the wild animals the LORD had made. He said to the woman, 'Did God really say, you must not eat from any tree in the garden?'" Satan's main method of attack in the beginning (and still today) was to attempt to place doubt in God's Word in the minds of men.

As Angela converses with Phil, he too uses the crafty techniques of Satan to try to get Angela to doubt God's Word. Biblical creationists are very aware that besides historical narrative the Bible uses literary techniques for communication. An aspect of any proper exegesis is to understand context and literary method. It is not logical thinking to attempt to distort those differences in biblical communication styles into a license for people to interpret the Bible any way they want. Phil illogically and incorrectly tries to influence Angela to believe that since the Bible sometimes uses metaphor, metaphorical interpretations can be called on at whim. The plain facts of the historical narrative of Genesis 1-11, and the other references to those chapters elsewhere in the Bible, do not allow for the insertion therein to include evolution and millions of years. Millions of years and evolution are nowhere found in the Bible.

Does Phil call God a liar when he says, "As we see here, Angela, there are some readings of Scripture that are simply not consistent with our expanding knowledge of God's creation"? Phil would probably say no, but his "deeper interpretations" are exactly that—interpretations based on atheistic and deistic presuppositions. And those who *really believe* in the religion of evolution are people who do not even believe there is a God as described in the Bible!

The goal of the AAAS is to convince Christians that evolutionary interpretations are science (meaning knowledge) while those biblical interpretations accepted by Christians who rely on God's Word are just religion. Phil was attempting to convince Angela that evolutionary philosophy can trump the Bible, and once she accepts that position, her Christian faith will slip into the realm of either inconsistency or else apostasy. One cannot accept interpretations based on atheistic and deistic presuppositions and still be able to accept or properly understand God's Word.

The mention of leviathan in the dialogue between Phil and Angela reminds me that there are other biblical references to that fearsome sea creature besides Psalm 104. For example, Psalm 74, Job 3, Job 41, and Isaiah 26 provide additional descriptive material that leads creationists, using biblical presuppositions, to conclude that Phil is incorrect when he describes leviathan as possibly a whale. Why would a supposedly Christian campus advisor provide students like Angela with *only* arguments for distrusting the more literal interpretation of the Bible? One would think that a true Christian advisor would, at the very least, provide the literal interpretation as at least an option when discussing origins with students. But alas, this hypothetical interaction between advisor and student is all too realistic, and it represents what would be expected where so many have been evolutionized by the culture and the academic environment that is totally controlled by people such as those with the bias of the AAAS.

CHRISTIANITY IN DARWIN'S TIME

The seamless blending of all knowledge

The authors of *The Evolution Dialogues* are to be commended for not portraying James Ussher as an idiot. Many anti-creationists and old-earthers have done this, which is always an indication of their ignorance concerning Bishop Ussher. Secularists may not be aware that Ussher's work, *The Annals of the World,* was republished in an easy-to-read English revision by Larry and Marion Pierce in 2003—the first major English revision since it was published in 1658. Historians should take advantage of the wealth of scholarly information in this book. The authors wrote in the Editor's Preface of the 2003 edition the following:

Ussher's *Annals of the World*

"The format used for the footnotes is explained in the bibliography at the end of this work. In most history books, it is very difficult to tell where the material came from. Separating the editorials from the facts would challenge even Solomon. This is not true of Ussher's work. It contains more than twelve thousand footnotes from secular sources and over two thousand quotes from the Bible or the Apocrypha. There is very little editorializing and most editorial comments come from the original writers themselves."

Biblical creationists would expect that Ussher's technique of seamlessly blending evidence from the Bible, (secular) history, and nature would still be the best way to understand any historical truth. Of course, this is not the belief of most of today's secular scholars and compromising liberal Christians who instead believe that the thoughts of man can supersede the plain reading of God's Word. One denomination of Protestants even has the motto, "We take the Bible seriously but not literally." I always wonder when I see that motto on a sign in front of a church, which particular parts of the Bible that they take seriously.

Often overlooked by secular historians and others is that Ussher is not the only one who arrived at a young age for the earth. The Septuagint arrived at a date of the creation at 5270 BC. The Jewish historian Josephus came up with a date of 5555 BC. And using the Bible as a resource, Kepler calculated 3993 BC and Martin Luther arrived at 3961 BC. In fact, anyone with the incentive can use the biblical chronologies in Genesis chapters 5 and 11 to arrive at their own date of creation. Yes, some apparent gaps and assumptions must be made, and this is why everyone does not come up with exactly the same date, but it will normally fall at less than 4500 BC. My calculations arrived at a date of 4114 BC for the Creation. That is a far cry from the evolutionary assumption of 4,600,000,000 BC.

The world as inferred from the Bible

The explanation in *The Evolution Dialogues* for "the world as inferred from the Bible" is basically correct so far as it goes. Genesis clearly describes God's special creation with plants made on Day 3, sea creatures and birds on Day 5, and land animals and humans on Day 6. The Bible plainly reads that living things were created "according to their kinds," and that God saw that everything He created was very good (Genesis 1:31). However, due to what is left out, *The Evolution Dialogues'* explanation is misleading in three ways:

1. The correct exegesis of Genesis is not read to imply that human beings held a special place in the creation only because they were made last. Humans hold a special place in creation primarily because God created humans in His own image (Genesis 1:27, 5:1), and God blessed them and directed them to rule over every living creature (Genesis 1:28). In addition, unlike all other lifeforms, God directly communicated with Adam and Eve in the Garden of Eden (Genesis 2:15-17, 3:8-19).

2. *The Evolution Dialogues* leaves out several important and critical events of Genesis chapters 1 through 11 that help to explain the world. Left out is the Fall of man when Eve was deceived and Adam chose to disobey God and eat of the forbidden fruit, thereby committing the original sin, which brought death and the curse to the "very good" creation (Genesis 3). Left out was the worldwide cataclysmic Flood, which was the result of "every inclination of the thoughts of his heart was only evil all the time." This evil resulted in God's judgment on mankind with only eight humans surviving and the whole creation suffering because of this disobedience (Genesis 6-9). And left out was God's action at the Tower of Babel when man's rebellion against God resulted in His confusing the languages of the people and scattering them throughout the globe (Genesis 11). It is not surprising that these events are left out of the Genesis explanation by evolutionists, but it is inexcusable for a book that purports to explain what the Bible says.

3. It is arguable as to how many Christian scholars elaborated on the "great chain of being." The important point is that the Greek "great chain of being" was a pantheistic philosophy with no basis in the Bible. Many ideas of men are incorrect, including some ideas of Christian scholars. A plain reading of Genesis explains that life was created "according to their kinds" and not according to some long chain of simple to complex organisms. Evolutionary and creationist scientists of the 19th century knew that even "simple" life was very complex.

Today we know that there is no such thing as "simple" life. It is contradictory for evolutionists to say creationists believed, "that God created each living kind in a unique act of special creation" (p. 39) and then say they believe that "God had started with simpler organisms and link by individual link had worked up to the creation of humanity." The majority of Bible believers of the 19th century believed as biblical creationists do today: There is no way to interpret the Bible to include simple to complex linkages for the creation of life.

Nevertheless, whatever the majority of biblical creationists believed in Darwin's time, it is clear today that the biblical truth matches the current true science on this matter. And that is that God's created kinds were provided at the time of creation (in DNA) with the ability to adapt (designed adaptability) to various environments, but that one kind cannot evolve into another kind because the information for this type of macro-evolutionary change is not in the DNA. There is no information that will allow dogs to evolve into cats, dinosaurs, or birds. Humans have been humans since the creation and will always be humans, even though they are degenerating due to birth defects, which are one result of the curse from the time of the Fall.

Natural philosophy and natural theology

The section of *The Evolution Dialogues* on "natural philosophy and natural theology" is well written, and I have no major issues with it. However, here again they left out some very important information. The design argument is easy to accept intuitively. Everyone knows from day-to-day experience how to tell designed objects from things that have their shape and structure due to chance interactions with the environment. William Paley's *Natural Theology* is, in large part, plain old common sense. In my Traveling Dinosaur and Fossil Museum is a "Design" section that contains a box with several randomly formed natural rocks and one Indian arrowhead. Even young children have no difficulty identifying the one designed rock in the display box.

Another example of how people will believe anything is the argument by evolutionists that although life is very complex and looks obviously designed, it really was not designed. They say that life's design came about due to time, chance, and the laws of matter. A specific example of this type of thinking is by well-known atheist/anti-Christian Richard Dawkins who wrote, "Biology is the study of complicated things that give the appearance of having been designed for a purpose."[7]

Why does Dawkins write that life only has "the appearance of having been designed for a purpose"? The reason is that he has presupposed that there is no God and so it must follow that life must have just happened. Dawkins attempts to convince others that he knows how design in life comes about by claiming, "Natural selection is the blind watchmaker, blind because it does not see ahead, does not plan consequences, has no purpose in view. Yet the living results of natural selection overwhelmingly impress us with the illusion of designed planning."[8]

Can you Find the Designed Rock?

I am not sure if Dawkins really believes that natural selection is the source for all design in living things, but his anti-Christian writing and speaking career has brought him a lot of fame and money. He has indeed convinced many that he does know what he is talking about. What he writes and says are stories, fairy tales actually. Natural selection can only select from what is available in the DNA of a lifeform. DNA is an information storage system similar to a set of encyclopedias or a computer flash drive. DNA cannot create new information any more than a set of encyclopedias can. It is more reasonable to believe that the information in the DNA was placed there by the Intelligent Designer in the beginning!

Natural selection cannot explain the creation of the universe, the creation of the solar system, the creation of the earth, or the creation of the first organic chemicals. How could a protein or a living cell be selected from a rock?

Scientists have discovered that the earth and life on our planet could not exist except for the clock-like coordination of many natural laws and constants. For example, if the sun were closer to earth, life could not exist. If the sun were farther away, life could not exist. If everything randomly evolved from nothing over time, why would there exist such laws of nature and the delicate balance of ecological processes we see on earth? These finely tuned processes are an indication of the intelligent design and providential grace of a loving God! In Job 34:14-15 we read, "If it were his [God's] intention and he withdrew his spirit and breath, all mankind would perish together and man would return to the dust."

In 1981, mathematicians Fred Hoyle and Chandra Wickramasinghe reached the conclusion from their calculations that it is impossible that life could result from time, chance, and the properties of matter. In fact, Hoyle said that believing life could come from time, chance, and the properties of matter was like believing that "a tornado sweeping through a junkyard might assemble a Boeing 747 from the materials therein."[9]

The law of biogenesis demands that life comes only from life and cells only come from cells. This law has never been observed to have been violated in nature or laboratory. Though they are often reluctant to admit it, evolutionists believe that at least once in the distant past the law of biogenesis was broken in nature (called *abiogenesis*), and that organic chemicals somehow evolved from inorganic chemicals (or life from a rock). This is also called *spontaneous generation* and must be accepted on blind faith with no solid scientific evidence. It is helpful to think of spontaneous generation this way. Imagine you have a living pet (say a dog) with you that suddenly dies. At the instant before it dies it has everything necessary for life. However, once it is dead it cannot be brought back to life except by a miraculous intervention. It is not our experience that dead things that were once living can come back to life. Yet a life form that just died would be the easiest thing to imagine coming back to life since it has all of the "stuff" it had the instant before when it was living. However, evolutionists believe that something that never had life somehow came to be alive on its own.

On page 43 of *The Evolution Dialogues* a statement is made that is very strange. They claimed that one criticism of Natural Theology was "that the evidence of God found in nature would not convince nonbelievers." In my experience, if any sort of evidence would convince nonbelievers to accept God it would be evidence from His Creation. At least this would be true for those people who are analytical thinkers like scientists, engineers, technicians, etc.

It is my observation that one of the shortcomings of most Christian youth programs today is that they regularly ignore young people who are analytical thinkers, so those kids end up leaving the church very early on. These youth leaders have no answers for these types of kids and they make little or no attempt to get the answers they need regarding the plain biblical teachings of Genesis 1-11 and what they are taught in the public schools and by the media about origins. The youth that get the attention are those who are interested in the arts, music, and social interactions.

This is what happened to me. I grew up in the church but was an evolutionist until age 40. I was unable to accept the accuracy and inerrancy of God's Word since there was no consistency between the Bible and the evolutionary dogma I was taught in my formal education. It was not possible to accept the Bible seriously in any aspect until I was shown that, by having the proper presuppositions, I could find the consistency between God's Word and God's Creation. I know scores of other biblical creationists today who would say the exact same thing convinced them; and the result of "seeing the light" was that they are now able to believe the Bible from the very first verse.

The AAAS goal is to convince people that a consistency can be found between evolution, millions of years, and the Bible. This is impossible unless the Bible is stripped of its underlying Truth and artificially replaced with atheistic and deistic philosophies. Any person who thinks that the Creator was scientifically ignorant is not likely to believe that He could provide the key to everlasting life!

Charles Darwin was required to read Paley's *Natural Theology* and stated that it was one of the books he most enjoyed in his formal education. Darwin was just as amazed by the human eye as was Paley and stated so in *The Origin of Species*. Since Darwin's time we have learned even more amazing facts about the human eye, some of which are:

> The eye is an incredibly complex organ that moves 100,000 times in an average day. Numerous muscles and tear ducts are in place to keep the eye constantly moist, protected, and functional. Our eyes process 1.5 million bits of information simultaneously and provide 80% of the sensory stimulation sent to the brain. They receive light images traveling at 186,000 miles per second through the iris, which opens or closes to let in just the right amount of light. These images travel through a lens, made of transparent cells, which focuses them on the retina at the back of the eyeball. The retina covers less than one square inch of surface, yet this square inch contains approximately 137 million light-sensitive receptor cells. Approximately 130 million are rod cells (designed specifically to see in black and white), and 7 million are cone cells (allowing color vision). Finally, the image is sent at a rate of 300 miles per hour to the brain for processing. How could all of this have come about by some step-by-step, random-chance evolutionary process?[10]

What is even more amazing to me than the human eye itself is what some people will say they believe. For example, Richard Dawkins has been able to publish numerous best selling books that attempt to refute the natural theology argument by saying in effect, "If it looks like a duck, walks like a duck, and quacks like a duck, it is obviously not a duck." I guess books of fantasy have always been popular; and Dawkins has found a way to make a living. It is a way to make a living but definitely not a God-honoring way to make a living! I pray he comes around to the truth soon or I fear he will face a terrible judgment.

William Paley (1743-1805) and his *Natural Theology* made sense in the 19th century and makes even more sense in the 21st. I say hurray for William Paley and for *Natural Theology!*

An evolving sense of history

The Bible tells us that Jesus Christ was and is God. Jesus himself said, "I am the way and the truth and the life. No one comes to the Father except through me" (John 14:6). Jesus also said, "I am the bread of life" (John 6:35), "before Abraham was born, I am" (John 8:58), "I am the light of the world" (John 8:12), "I am the gate for the sheep" (John 10:7), "I am the good shepherd" (John 10:11), "I am the resurrection and the life" (John 11:25), and "I am the true vine" (John 15:1). Real Christians believe these things are true, and it would not be consistent for them to accept beliefs that are contrary to Jesus' own statements.

The Evolution Dialogues documents many Christian heretical beliefs that came to be during the 18th and 19th centuries. That does not mean that these beliefs are valid or that they (e.g. "higher criticism") have not all been soundly refuted by conservative scholarship. In chapter one of *The Creation Dialogues* I noted that scriptural geologists such as George Young provided convincing contemporary refutations to uniformitarianism and millions of years. The day-age theory, the gap theory, and other compromising explanations required by evolution for the straight-forward narrative of Genesis 1-11 are shown to be unnecessary and bogus by present day creation science. And no matter what the consensus or majority of western scientists believed at the end of the 19th century, those who accepted the concept that religious speculation and faith statements must be kept separate from their empirical studies and scientific conclusions were totally disingenuous when it came to evolutionary theories. Darwin, Spencer, Wallace, T.H. Huxley, and the other evolutionists of the 19th century never had a single empirical observation that showed one kind of life evolving into another kind. No subsequent evolutionist has had any better luck at devising or conducting a scientific experiment that proves even the possibility of either abiogenesis or macro evolution. This is all undeniable evidence that evolution is religion, must be accepted by faith, and therefore is not science. Christians have a historically based and verified faith. Why would anyone want to replace a faith with strong evidence for its veracity with a faith based on atheistic speculations and philosophies? That is exactly what the AAAS would have Christians do.

The history that was evolving in the 19th century, which attempted to insert evolution and millions of years into the Bible, was evolving only in the minds of men darkened in their understanding (Ephesians 4:18).

Darwin's religious views

As mentioned, I do not believe Darwin would have published his *Origin of Species* book if he had not been pressured by Hooker and Lyell to do so and if he had not accepted Lyell's uniformitarianism. Darwin was not an evil person in the sense that Hitler, Stalin, or Pol Pot were, but was driven away from the God of the Bible by the influence of his "free thinking" father and grandfather, and by his observations of death, disease, and suffering. Darwin was not alone in not being able to understand how a loving God could allow such misery in the world. Today, even Bible-believing Christians have difficulty understanding why there is so much death and suffering in this life.

Many people have rejected Christianity in part because of the suffering in the world. The late Charles Templeton published a book entitled *Farewell to God* in 1996. In this book he described his slide into unbelief and his rejection of the faith. At one time Templeton was a famous evangelist and colleague of Billy Graham. Templeton was once listed among those "best used of God" by the National Association of Evangelicals. In his book Templeton wrote, "Why does God's grand design require creatures with teeth designed to crush spines or rend flesh, claws fashioned to seize and tear, venom to paralyze, mouths to suck blood, coils to constrict and smother—even expandable jaws so that prey may be swallowed whole and alive?...Nature is in Tennyson's vivid phrase, 'red [with blood] in tooth and claw,' and life is a carnival of blood." Templeton then concludes, "How could a loving and omnipotent God create such horrors as we have been contemplating?"[11]

We earlier learned the Bible says that God created everything and then judged it to be "very good" (Genesis 1:31). God originally created a perfect world. People and animals ate plants, not other animals (Genesis 1:29-30). There was no violence or pain in this "very good" world. What happened?

The answer is provided in Genesis chapter 3 where we learn of the fall into sin by Adam and Eve that resulted in the curse and death. We also learn in Genesis 3:15 (the protoevangel) of God's plan for redemption of His creation. Therefore, the Bible provides a consistent explanation for death and suffering (sin) and also God's solution (Jesus).

On the other hand, if one believes in millions of years, then this world has always been a deadly place. The question is naturally asked is, "Who or what caused the cancer, other diseases, and violence represented in the fossil record?" How do biblical creationists explain this? The Bible has an answer that is consistent with the evidence, and that is the Fall and then the worldwide Flood of Genesis 6-9. As Ken Ham has said, "If there really was a worldwide flood, what would the evidence be? How about billions of dead things buried in rock layers laid down by water all over the earth"? As a result of man's rebellion into sin and God's judgment at the Garden of Eden, God has given mankind a taste of life without all of His sustaining presence and a world that is running down; a world full of death and suffering. From the perspective of the Bible, death is not something that has always been around, that is good, and that will always be around. In 1 Corinthians 15:26 death is described as "the last enemy." So if evolution is the true explanation of origins, then death was normal and widespread before men evolved. But if death preceded man and was not a result of Adam's sin, then sin is a fiction. If sin is a fiction, then there is no need for a Savior, and Christ's redemptive work on the cross was for nothing. It is abundantly clear that evolution and millions of years are in no way compatible with Biblical Christianity! If you remove the explanations in the Bible for the need for God to come down to die for the sin of man, you are left with a Jesus who is a liar and lunatic. What kind of religion is that? It is the religion with which the AAAS would like to convince Christians they should be content.

Even with all of this death and suffering, the great hope of Christians exists in the gospel message. In John 3:16-18 we are encouraged, "For God so loved the world that he gave his only begotten Son, that whoever believes in him shall not perish but have eternal life. For God did not send his Son into the world to condemn the world, but to save the world through him. Whoever believes in him is not condemned, but whoever does not believe stands condemned already because he has not believed in the name of God's one and only Son."

Christians have found that there can be "good" in this life that results from suffering:

1. Suffering can "perfect" us, or make us mature in the image of Christ (Job 23:10, Hebrews 5:8-9).
2. Suffering can help some to come to know Christ.
3. Suffering can make us more able to empathize with and comfort others who suffer.

It is not clear how much time Darwin spent considering the Bible's explanation for death and suffering, but he, like many others of the 19th century, eventually chose to ignore it.

FURTHER READING

1. Morris, Henry, *The Long War Against God*, Master Books, 2000.
2. Morris, Henry, *Many Infallible Proofs*, Master Books, 1996.
3. Paley, William, *Natural Theology*, Oxford University Press, 2006.
4. Ussher, James, *The Annals of the World*, Master Books, 2003.

CHAPTER 3
THE THEORY OF EVOLUTION

ANGELA'S STORY

THAT THE THEORY of evolution has no foundation other than in fantasy can clearly be seen in chapter three of *The Evolution Dialogues*! The authors use some 21 pages in order to provide "stories," speculations and hypotheses, with the purpose of attempting to convince the unwary of the viability of this theory, a theory that is supposed to prove how "all species living and extinct are related to each other" (p. 54). Microevolution (variability) occurs in lifeforms. The point of contention is macroevolution, which requires new abilities, new information, and increasing complexity. It does not occur, has not occurred, and cannot occur.

In chapter 3 Angela reveals that she has been told in her biology class that the theory of evolution includes certain foundational concepts. These concepts include *extinction*, *species population counts*, *the balance of nature*, and *symbiotic relationships*. However, extinction is not evolutionary change! Extinction means that at a certain time in history a lifeform exists and at a later time that lifeform has died off. Extinction provides no mechanism for macro-evolutionary change. Species population counts, the balance of nature, and symbiotic relationships are not evolution either. Angela's discussion with Dr. Dunbar in the chapter 3 prologue is a smokescreen with not a single scientific fact applicable to the issue of macroevolution.

In chapter two of *The Creation Dialogues*, I provided the biblical explanation for Angela's question brought up again when she asks, "Why would he [God] set up nature to be so cruel?" The answer I gave was that He didn't! It was mankind's sin that brought death and suffering into the creation. The current status of the universe is but a remnant of the original "very good" creation. Believers have been promised in God's Word that this situation is not permanent and a perfect creation will one day be restored.

Nevertheless, evolution has great difficulty explaining the many symbiotic and irreducibly complex relationships that science has discovered. It makes more sense (especially to the consistent Christian) that these relationships are the result of design provided by the Creator rather than blind and brainless evolutionary processes for which there is no known mechanism.

Yes the story of evolution told by the dialogue between Angela and Dr. Dunbar is as fictional and phony as the one fabricated by the authors about Angela's procedures for installing the plant shelf with the "screw gun."

Let us take a closer look at these evolutionary stories as they have been expanded in chapter three.

THE THEORY OF EVOLUTION

Evolution in action
Natural selection
Other evolutionary mechanisms
Microevolution and macroevolution
Evidence for evolution
Focus of current research

In *The Evolution Dialogues,* chapter three begins with three "stories" that are supposed to demonstrate the theory of evolution. After these stories are concluded, another ten attempts at demonstrating the same idea are added. Each and every one of the stories is an example of interpretations based on the atheistic and deistic presuppositions that we have been pointing out in *The Creation Dialogues.*

In "story 1" are found at least two interpretations that are definitely not facts. It is *not* a fact that *Dilong paradoxus* is the ancestor of *Tyrannosaurus rex.* It is *not* a fact that birds are biological heirs of dinosaurs. Both of these conclusions are interpretations based on evolutionary paleontology presuppositions. These interpretations rely on the presupposition that homology (structural similarities) prove evolution. Evolutionists always presuppose common ancestors, while creationists normally presuppose a Common Designer. Specifically, biblical creationists know that birds did not evolve from dinosaurs because birds were created on day 5 before animals, which were created on day 6.

I devoted a year to the study of the "Poster Child for Evolution," *Archaeopteryx,* using biblical creationist presuppositions and came to the conclusion that *Archaeopteryx was not a bird;* but since it had indications of dinosaur characteristics in almost all aspects, was probably a fraud. The details of my original research are available in a 2-hour-long DVD entitled *"Archaeopteryx: What Was It?"* This illustrates the importance of presuppositions since some evolutionist and creationist scientists believe that *Archaeopteryx* was a bird. In this case, the agreement existed because those creationists who believe that *Archaeopteryx* was a bird do so because they have (unwittingly?) accepted evolutionary presuppositions.

The authors of *The Evolution Dialogues* often use the phrase, "scientists believe." I suggest that in discussions of evolution that the adjective "some" always be added to that phrase, making the statements read, "*some* scientists believe." Of course creation scientists are at odds with these scientists, but evolutionary scientists often disagree among themselves. This is to be expected when the "science" is based on a fantasy.

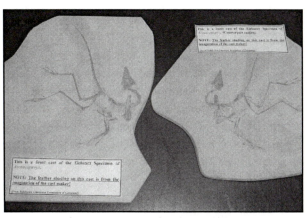

Archaeopteryx Casts of Eichstatt Specimen

Time after time the examples provided by evolutionists are examples of microevolution or speciation. The AAAS authors admit this on pages 59-60 when they discuss dogs and Darwin's finches, but cannot quite leave it at that when they write, "The study of the Galapagos Island finches has documented not only micro evolutionary trends in beak size but also a macro evolutionary trend…" The finches at Galapagos started out as finches, changed to finches, and are still changing to slightly different finches. This is *not* the evolution that proves that, "all species living and extinct are related to each other."

None of the examples provided by the authors "illustrate[s] the variety of ways that scientists today are accumulating evidence to test the theory of evolution." No, they are examples of micro-evolutionary experiments, and the macroevolution these experimenters promote must be imagined. And, as discussed earlier, the insurmountable problem with that exercise is the changes are headed down the track in the wrong direction! The experiments show not evolutionary progression, but rather *de*volutionary changes.

If only the faith in God of the average Christian were as strong as is the faith of evolutionists in their god (naturalism). On page 54 we read of "the accumulation of many small, incremental changes to traits, handed down through different lines of descendants over millions of years." But the fossil record only shows abrupt appearance and stasis, and evolutionists know this. Those evolutionists who are willing to admit the facts have been forced to develop other hypotheses such as punctuated equilibrium, which we read about on page 68 of *The Evolution Dialogues*. "According to one hypothesis, termed punctuated equilibrium, a species that has been stable for millions of years evolves into new lineages in a period as brief as a few tens of thousand of years." I doubt the originators of that hypothesis (Gould and Eldridge) would agree with the authors that punctuated equilibrium applies only "under certain circumstances." The abrupt appearance and stasis of the fossil record exists throughout and is not only in certain circumstances. The late Stephen Jay Gould wrote,

> The extreme rarity of transitional forms in the fossil record persists as the trade secret of paleontology. The evolutionary trees that adorn our textbooks have data only at the tips and nodes of their branches; the rest is inference, however reasonable, not the evidence of fossils.
>
> Paleontologists have paid an exorbitant price for Darwin's argument. We fancy ourselves as the only true students of life's history, yet to preserve our favored account of evolution by natural selection we view our data as so bad that we never see the very process we profess to study.
>
> The history of most fossil species includes two features particularly inconsistent with gradualism.
>
> 1. *Stasis.* Most species exhibit no directional change during their tenure on earth. They appear in the fossil record looking much the same as when they disappear; morphological change is usually limited and directionless.
> 2. *Sudden appearance.* In any local area, a species does not arise gradually by the steady transformation of its ancestors; it appears all at once and 'fully formed.'
>
> If gradualism is more a product of Western thought than a fact of nature, then we should consider alternative philosophies of change to enlarge our realm of constraining prejudices. In the Soviet Union, for example, scientists are trained with a very different philosophy of change—the so-called dialectical laws, reformulated by Engels from Hegel's philosophy. The dialectical laws are explicitly punctuational… Eldredge and I were fascinated to learn that most Russian paleontologists support a model very similar to our punctuated equilibria. The connection cannot be accidental.[12]

Evolution is so pliable that we can believe in "the accumulation of many small, incremental changes" over millions of years and at the same time "the evolution into new lineages in a brief period." Both of these beliefs are based not on evidence, but on a lack of evidence (read Gould's quote again if you don't see this immediately). Again we see that the evolution seen by the men of evolutionary faith is presupposed and not proven; and Gould believed the way he did primarily because he was a Marxist. His atheistic philosophy drove his conclusions further away from God instead of toward God.

The authors wrote that the study of "fruit flies may lead to a better understanding of evolution's time frames," yet "a century of fruit fly experiments, involving 3,000 consecutive generations, gives absolutely no basis for believing that any natural or artificial process can cause an increase in complexity and viability."[13]

Theodosius Dobzhansky wrote:

Most mutants which arise in any organism are more or less disadvantageous to their possessors. The classical mutants obtained in Drosophila [the fruit fly] usually show deterioration, breakdown, or disappearance of some organs. Mutants are known which diminish the quantity or destroy the pigment in the eyes, and in the body reduce the wings, eyes, bristles, legs. Many mutants are, in fact, lethal to their possessors. Mutants which equal the normal fly in vigor are a minority, and mutants that would make a major improvement of the normal organization in the normal environments are unknown.[14]

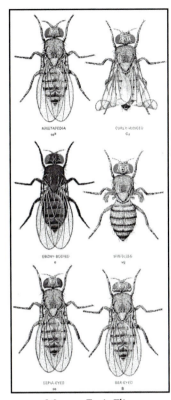

Mutant Fruit Flies

So we can subject these poor flies to all kinds of external and internal substances and actions and, after thousands of generations, they are still flies, albeit usually very bad-off flies. These experiments have no way to lead to better understanding of macro-evolutionary timeframes because there is no macro-evolution taking place.

Another indication of the falsity of the evolutionary faith is the use of "the tree of life" analogy. Evolutionists know, as Gould wrote above, that there is no such thing. Creationists would say that there is a "forest of life" or a "lawn of life," but there is definitely no evidence for a "tree of life" as sketched by Darwin. I'll discuss this topic of phylogenetic trees more when we get into cladistics.

On page 63 of *The Evolution Dialogues* we read, "Homologies provide more evidence for relatedness." This is a total understatement so far as the beliefs of evolutionists. For paleontologists, their life's work is based almost totally on homology. Evolutionary paleontologists, believe that homology is all that is needed to prove evolution from common ancestors. That this is true is clear from their published work, which almost always starts with the "fact" of similarity in structure being equal to proof of common descent. Most books on paleontology do not even bother to state this presupposition. Creation scientists, on the other hand, believe that their argument for a Common Designer easily trumps the evolutionist paradigm. Evolutionists hold by faith to the postulate that the wings of a bat, the flippers of a dolphin, and the arms of a man are homologous organs and have evolved from the paired fins of a fish ancestor.

A strong acknowledgement of the inability of homology to scientifically support evolutionary philosophy is the movement away from the standard terminology, which in the past has denoted *simple* to *complex* gradual evolutionary changes. Noted dinosaur paleontologist Dr. Peter Dodson concluded:

> Notice that I made these statements…without resorting to the word *primitive*. I also avoided using the word *advanced*…What is going on here? While valiantly resisting the assaults of post-modernism, scientific language, alas, is not immune to the dynamism of linguistic evolution. The terms *primitive* and *advanced* are no longer 'politically correct' and so must be expunged from our vocabulary. They are to be replaced by the terms *basal* or *generalized* and *derived*, thereby avoiding unfortunate connotations of superiority or inferiority.[15]

The reason why there are similarities in the inventions of mankind is these similarities are forced due to the requirement to accomplish the functions for which the inventions were made in the first place. Similarly, I believe that God used similar designs to accomplish similar functions in various lifeforms in His creation. Of course, His capabilities would far exceed any that man could ever formulate. "Great is our Lord and mighty in power; his understanding has no limits" (Psalm 147:5). "Who has known the mind of the Lord? Or who has been his counselor?" (Romans 11:34).

The atheistic and deistic presuppositions of evolution require a commitment to naturalism and a rejection of God. This is not a commitment to science; it is a commitment to a false philosophy.

On page 64 of *The Evolution Dialogues* is written, "A sufficient number of such [transitional] fossils have been found to document the evolutionary line that descends from primitive jawless fish to sharks, skates, and rays; from early land mammals to whales; from dinosaurs to birds; from primates to modern *Homo sapiens*, and down through many other lines of macro evolutionary change." I have been looking for transitional fossils for decades and have not found any in museums or in the literature. I have seen a few in cartoons, but we know that those are only from the minds of the cartoonists. Remember what Stephen Jay Gould wrote about these transitions?

A true transitional fossil is one that exhibits an in-process change in structure. A fossil showing a limb in the process of changing from a fin to a leg would be a transitional fossil. It requires tremendous mental gymnastics to be able to visualize how such a creature would ever survive to pass on its new features to the next generation! The only place where these types of transitional fossils exist is in the minds of evolutionists. The fossil record does not provide any evidence of true transitional forms. If evolution were true, there should be millions of these transitional forms. What we find *instead* is, as Gould wrote, stasis and abrupt appearance. This is exactly opposite to what the evolution model predicts, but exactly what the creation model predicts. After a billion fossils have been found and catalogued over the past 200 years, it should be clear that transitional forms are not found because they never existed. Darwin's greatest fear has been realized and his theory is garbage.

As I have visited secular natural history museums over the past few years, I have noticed that the old "tree of life" diagrams and time charts are slowly disappearing. This is because of the lack of transitional fossils. There is no way to place lifeforms on the trees except at the tips and nodes of the branches, which has become philosophically unsatisfactory. Therefore, secular scientists have begun using a different phylogenetic classifying system called cladistics. This is designed to replace the Linnaean taxonomy system that has been commonly in use for centuries. Cladistics

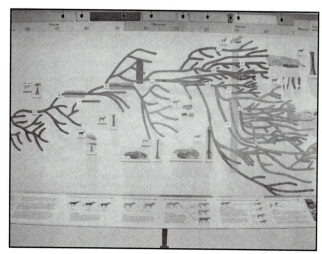

Condon Museum Phylogenetic Diagram

allows for the artificial determination of supposed ancestral relationships based totally on feature similarities between organisms. While lending itself nicely to computer analysis, each relationship is totally artificial and not based on any biological reality, such as from the fossil record. Because of this artificial relationship between lifeforms, cladistics is still controversial. Cladistics is almost exclusively being used today by dinosaur paleontologists since they usually have so little to work with (only bones, skulls, claws, and teeth). Cladograms are a great admission of the fact of the presupposition of evolution; and cladistics is clearly seen to have been devised in order to allow for the evolutionary common descent classifications that the living and fossil evidence does *not* show.

On their website, The American Museum of Natural History in New York City uses American coins (a penny, a nickel, a dime, and a quarter) to demonstrate to school children how cladistics works. However, if one changes the features of the coins that are selected from those given by the example, one finds that the cladogram also completely changes. That is, the "progressive" relationships of the coins to each other change. This is another way to see that cladistics is an artificial categorization method. Cladistics has been forced into evolutionary dinosaur paleontology by the lack of transitional fossils and by the continuing need for the evolutionist paradigm to accept the (false) presupposition that homology proves evolution.[16]

Creation scientist Dr. John Morris summarizes his decades of study of the fossil record:

We see that the fossil record is a record quite different from that presented in support of evolution. Each basic plant and animal type appeared abruptly and fully functional, and then experienced stasis throughout its tenure. Each type was complex and distinct from the start, without having descended from some other ancestral type, particularly from a less complex type.

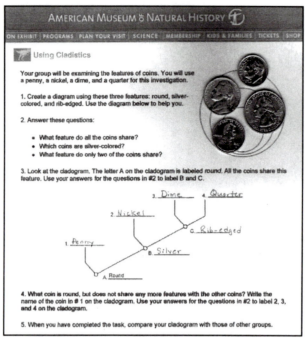

Cladogram with One Set of Assumptions

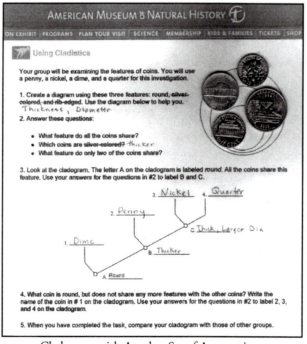

Cladogram with Another Set of Assumptions

All basic types which have ever lived were present at the start, and while some have subsequently gone extinct, no new basic types have appeared since the beginning. We have reason to believe substantially all basic forms which ever lived have been found as fossils.

A general rule is that the fossils extend through lengthy stratigraphic range with little or no change. Most of the fossils are remains of marine invertebrates, found in catastrophic deposits, often in death poses with an incomplete ecosystem present. These predominately marine fossils are almost all found on the continents, not in the ocean.

The fossil record is thus quite incompatible with evolution and uniformitarianism, but remarkably consistent with the biblical record: Creation of all things in perfect form and function, the curse on all things due to man's rebellion, and the Great Flood of Noah's day which first destroyed and then renovated the entire planet.

Creation thinking predicts the evidence, while evolution must distort and flex the evidence and its position to accommodate it.[17]

In conclusion, there is a lot of (mostly public) money being spent to keep evolutionary scientists busy. And, as mentioned earlier, a lot is at stake in both careers and fame. But the actual science being done is, for the most part, about as productive as was the work of the alchemists of the Middle Ages.

"Do you not know? Have you not heard? The LORD is the everlasting God, the Creator of the ends of the earth. He will not grow tired or weary, and his understanding no one can fathom. He gives strength to the weary and increases the power of the weak. Even youths grow tired and weary, and young men stumble and fall; but those who hope in the LORD will renew their strength. They will soar on wings like eagles; they will run and not grow weary, they will walk and not be faint" (Isaiah 40:28-31).

FURTHER READING

1. Brown, Walt, *In the Beginning: Compelling Evidence for Creation and the Flood*, Center for Scientific Creation, 2001.
2. DeYoung, Donald, *Dinosaurs and Creation*, Baker Books, 2000.
3. Gish, Duane, *Evolution: the Fossils Still Say No!* ICR, 1995.
4. Ham, Ken, *The Lie: Evolution*, Master Books, 1987.
5. Malone, Bruce, *Search for the Truth*, SFTT Publications, 2003.
6. Mitchell, J.D., *Homology from an Engineer's Perspective*, CEC, 2007.
7. Werner, Carl, *Living Fossils—Evolution: The Grand Experiment, vol. 2*, New Leaf Press, 2008.

INITIAL RESPONSES TO DARWIN'S THEORY

ANGELA'S STORY

IN CHAPTER 4, THE step-by-step evolutionary indoctrination of Angela continues. There is no new philosophic justification introduced in this chapter for Christians to believe in Darwinian evolution. In fact, the repetition is more than just trite and Angela's "campus ministry" advisor, Phil Compton, is represented to have little knowledge of the foundational basis for Christianity, i.e. the second person of the triune God, Jesus Christ.

Christianity is not just "believing in (a) god." Instead, Christianity is believing in Jesus Christ, the person that the biblical account takes 66 books to reveal. Those Christians who are influenced to compromise their beliefs so as to be compatible with the position of *The Evolution Dialogues* (and the AAAS) will, as I have been emphasizing, need to logically reject Jesus Christ as Lord and Savior. This is why biblical creationists are so adamant that Christians must understand what they are getting into when attempting to mix naturalism with their faith.

The truth is *not* as stated in chapter 4 by Phil when he says, "I'm saying that there is nothing inherent in evolution that is antagonistic to Christian belief." If we understand what is meant by the word "evolution" when used as a description of "particles to people" by the authors of *The Evolution Dialogues* and the AAAS, we are forced to logically throw out the Bible from Christianity. If the Bible is thrown out, Jesus is "the baby that goes out with the bath water." And when Jesus is thrown out, it is my contention that what is left is not Christianity.

Evolutionists believe that Thomas Henry Huxley's reported response to Bishop Wilberforce was "a great victory of the evolutionary argument over the religious."[18] Phil indicates the same attitude when he recounts the old myth for Angela. But just what would this mean if it were true that Huxley's supposed argument was, or is now, victorious? It would mean that the concept of man evolving from rocks, to pond scum, to fish, to apes, and finally to a conscious human being would be an idea superior to, "so God created man in his own image, in the image of God he created him; male and female he created them" (Genesis 1:27). It would mean that Jesus was just an ignorant man and not the Creator God when He said, "Haven't you heard that at the beginning the Creator made them male and female" (Matthew 19:4). People can and do believe anything, and the idea of man evolving from rocks is very popular. However, this concept is not in any way compatible with the Bible, and why knowledgeable Christians would want to incorporate the idea into their faith is beyond comprehension.

Finally, Angela says, "God's motivation. I still would like to understand that." I can only say that this is another indication that Angela (and those she hypothetically represents) does not take the Bible seriously or perhaps has not studied it. It is only by studying God's Word that one can learn and then understand God' motivation. That study will result in seeing that God's motivation is driven by His unfathomable love for us!

INITIAL RESPONSES TO DARWIN'S THEORY

A topic of personal interest

The authors of *The Evolution Dialogues* are correct to say that *The Origin of Species* accomplished two things:

1. It raised doubt about God having a personal relationship to mankind.
2. It raised doubt about the source of human morality.

For centuries, most people, and Christians especially, understood the straight forward message of the Bible concerning these two topics. It was clear that God made man in His image and that man was not able to determine right from wrong without God's commandments. And thinking people would, in the late 19th century, be very concerned about these very important issues since they could clearly see that they could be interpreted to refute, or at least make irrelevant, the teachings of God's Word.

Two hundred years have passed and the situation has not changed. Accepting Darwinism and its need for millions of years of macro-evolutionary changes either refutes the Bible or makes it irrelevant. Of course, that is the issue! *The Evolution Dialogues'* position is that this way of thinking is a good thing and should be acceptable to Christians. *The Creation Dialogues'* position is that this is heresy and an unacceptable compromise that calls God a liar and tends to undermine the Christian faith.

I always get a kick out of the sensitivity of evolutionists to the phrase "monkey-to-man." They complain, "Oh, it is not correct to say that we advocate the evolution of man from monkeys." Well, whether we call our supposed evolutionary ancestors hominids, apes, or something else, we can be sure that any "scientific" depictions of these ancestors would never be identified by any five-year-old child as anything other than a monkey. So to be affable we can say that we have not evolved from monkeys but from a lifeform that "looks" like a monkey.

Rejection

Qualified acceptance

I believe that the authors have misinterpreted the position of Charles Lyell concerning Darwin's theory of evolution (on page 78). In *The Evolution Dialogues* we read, "However, there were aspects of Darwin's theory that Lyell found difficult to reconcile with his beliefs about humankind's special position in God's creation." In my personal study of Lyell's writings I have come to the following entirely different conclusions:

1. Lyell was not a Biblical Christian. His writings indicate that he was a deist or perhaps Unitarian.
2. Among Lyell's goals was to minimize or totally erase the influence of Genesis chapters 1-11 on his intellectual society. In fact, I'm not sure he believed any of the books in the Bible attributed to Moses by most biblical scholars. He resented the fact that many still accepted the words of Moses over his "scientific" opinions.
3. Lyell did not dispute aspects of Darwin's theory on theological grounds. Instead he disputed them on naturalistic grounds.
4. By the time of Lyell's death in 1875, he had accepted most of Darwin's positions on evolution by natural selection.

It is not a correct interpretation of history to place Lyell in the "qualified acceptance" category for Darwin's theory as have the authors. Darwin and Lyell were "two peas in a pod" and together can be given most of the credit (blame!) for the evolutionary philosophy that developed in the 19th century and continues to this day. Charles Darwin would likely be totally unknown today if it hadn't been for Charles Lyell's writings and Lyell's personal influence on Darwin throughout their lives.

Enthusiastic support

I don't know if it is accurate to call Thomas Henry Huxley "Darwin's Bulldog" but it would be very accurate to call him "Evolution's Bulldog." Huxley epitomizes the men of scientific bent of the 19th century who took exception to the control of the Anglican Church over academia and were determined to wrest that control away. In fact, Huxley may have had more to do with that tilt of the scientific balance away from the Church to the secular than any other one man in Western history.

It is typical of believers in the worldview of naturalism to identify their way of thinking as "reason-based." This type of reason believes that everything came from nothing and that life evolved from rocks. While Christians are often painted as having thinking not based on reason, in reality the truth is the opposite. Our religion is one that is based on a Book that has proven reliable over many centuries, and that presents many specific and accurate prophecies. These prophecies alone are excellent justification for people to accept the Bible as reasonable in every respect. Since the Creator is outside of time (the inventor of time actually), He can make 100% accurate prophecies that point to the highest possible standard of reason. Naturalism's reason is man-based while Christianity's reason is God-based.

Biblical creationists do not argue that there is no evidence for natural selection, but that there is no correct, scientific interpretation of this evidence that proves macroevolution or an age of millions of years for the Earth.

Asa Gray and many others have been able to advance a compromise belief in theistic evolution. Theistic evolution is a belief that attempts to insert biological evolution and millions of years into the Genesis story and instead ends up throwing the Bible out. The following discussion and comparisons will make that clear.

ORIGIN BELIEF COMPARISON

To illustrate my point regarding theistic evolution I have chosen fifteen different topics of the origins controversy. I will discuss each of these topics with respect to three different belief systems, which are: "Biblical creation" (BC) based on the Bible, "molecules-to-man evolution" (MME) based on the beliefs of people like those in the AAAS, and "theistic evolution" (TE) based on the beliefs of those who try to combine MME with the Bible.

Topic #1: Where did life come from?

This is an easy question to answer for BC since the Bible is consistent in stating that life was created by God in the beginning. The MME position is that life evolved from rocks, which were the result of the explosions of stars. The TE position is that God somehow created life in some simple form, and then it evolved over long periods of time to the present situation. There is no agreement here between BC and TE except there is a God. The BC God is a personal God while the TE God cannot be considered personal when it comes to the creation of life.

Topic #2: How did lifeform variety come about?

The BC position is that God created the various original kinds of life with information in its DNA sufficient to allow much variation; and with the purpose to allow for foreseen needs for adaptation to changing environmental and ecological conditions. The MME and TE positions are identical; they believe natural selection and mutations can explain all variety from simple common ancestors.

Topic #3: How did man originate?

The BC position is that God made man in the beginning from the dust of the Earth and then made woman from man. The MME and TE positions are identical, and that is that man evolved from ape-like ancestors.

Topic #4: How many races are there?

The BC position is that there is only one race—the human race (see Acts 17:26). The MME and TE positions are identical, stating that there are four races.

Topic #5: What is the origin of the Earth and the universe?

The BC position is that God created everything in the beginning over a period of six ordinary days. The MME position is that everything was made from nothing as the result of a big bang. Similarly, the TE position is that God used a big bang to create everything.

Saturn and Some of its Moons

Topic #6: How are the biblical days of creation explained?

The BC position is that the days of creation are ordinary approximately 24 hour days. The MME and TE positions are identical, namely that the days of creation are a myth.

Topic #7: What is the age of the Earth?

The BC position is that the Earth is about 6,000 years old. The MME and TE positions are identical that the earth is very old with a current estimate of 4.6 billion years.

Topic #8: What about dinosaurs?

The BC position is that dinosaurs were created by God on day six along with all of the other animals and with man. The MME and TE positions are identical that dinosaurs evolved and then went extinct about 65 million years ago.

Topic #9: What about death, disease, and suffering?

The BC position is that death, disease, and suffering are a punishment for sin, which resulted from the Fall in the Garden of Eden as described in Genesis. The MME and TE positions are identical that death, disease, and suffering have always been a part of life and are, in fact, good because they are what forces evolution (survival of the fittest) and the progress of life toward better and better organisms.

Topic #10: Is there a moral authority?

The BC position is that the Bible is the authoritative and inerrant moral authority directly from God. The MME position is that there really is no moral authority except for what may have evolved for survival or what may match each person's personal preferences. The TE position is that the Bible may offer some moral guidance for certain cases as determined by each person's personal preferences.

Topic #11: What is the general view of the Bible?

As stated above the BC position is that the Bible is authoritative and inerrant. The MME position is that the Bible is just another man-made book that may be acceptable for some people to read for lifestyle advice. The TE view is all over the map, which should be expected since the Bible is authoritative only on certain issues.

Topic #12: What do the geologic layers represent?

The BC position is that the geologic layers are a result of the year-long cataclysmic worldwide Flood as described in

Geologic Layers in the Grand Canyon

Genesis 6-9. The MME and TE positions are identical, namely that the geologic layers are evidence for millions of years of earth history.

Topic #13: What about the Genesis Flood?

The BC position is that it happened exactly as described in the Bible, was cataclysmic, and covered the surface of the entire earth. The MME position is that the Genesis Flood is myth and the TE position is that, if it happened at all, it was a small local flood in the Middle East.

Topic #14: What is the fossil record?

The BC position is that the fossil record is evidence for God's judgment and the Genesis Flood, where all land animals and all people except for the eight that were on Noah's Ark were destroyed. The MME and TE positions are identical, namely that the fossil record is evidence for evolution.

Tyrannosaurus rex Skeleton at Museum of the Rockies

Topic #15: What was Noah's Ark?

The BC position is that Noah's Ark was a large barge-like vessel with the best possible design to survive a huge flood. The MME and TE positions are identical that Noah's Ark was a modest vessel or perhaps another myth.

An analysis of the three positions shows that the BC and TE positions on origins do not agree on any of the topics! This means that since the BC positions are taken consistently and directly from the Bible, that those holding to the TE positions have, in effect, thrown out the Bible. Also, it should be a concern to every Christian that the MME and TE positions are identical on ten out of the fifteen topics. It was a great concern for me prior to 1984 when, as a nominal Christian, I unsuccessfully attempted to understand the Bible from a theistic evolutionary viewpoint. Theistic evolution is just as bankrupt as is atheistic evolution, which should be expected since they are both based on the same presuppositions.

Evolution of scientific and public opinion

The authors of *The Evolution Dialogues* write on page 81, "A main concern was whether the Earth was old enough to accommodate evolutionary history. Another concern had to do with the many gaps in the fossil record. Such concerns were eventually overcome by new evidence from the fields of geology and paleontology."

So, nearly halfway through the book we see that the pro-evolution authors are aware of the major problems of evolutionary theory. In *The Creation Dialogues* I have made it clear that these major problems have not been overcome by any scientific evidences. Instead they have been overcome by faith using no God, everything from nothing, evolution from common ancestors over billions of years, and homology proving evolution presuppositions. With those presuppositions as a foundation, any evidence from the fields of geology and paleontology would have to be interpreted as proving evolution and millions of years. As of today, there still exist no true transitional fossils and so all of the "many gaps in the fossil record" are still an insurmountable problem for evolutionists.

As of today, the old age of the earth is just presupposed and not proven. What we know about the origin of life and variation in lifeforms tells us that even 4.6 billion years is not enough time for macroevolution to occur. This is because macroevolution is impossible without the necessary information needed to allow for any kind-to-new kinds of changes. No, the information is not in the genome, and the locomotive is headed down the track in the wrong direction!

You may ask, why are these points about evolution from the biblical creationist view being repeated so often in *The Creation Dialogues*? The answer is that the points are provided no more often than are the opposite viewpoints in *The Evolution Dialogues*. A favorite method of argument for the evolutionary view is, if the argument is not accepted at first, keep repeating it with more and more emphasis until the message is blasted at top volume. It is only fair to be able to offer a defense whenever the biblical view is attacked.

Evolving Christian responses

The response from other religions

Since *The Evolution Dialogues* is fundamentally an attack on the Biblical Christian worldview, I will not comment on the authors' opinions regarding the Roman Catholic Church, Judaism, Islam, Buddhism, Confucianism, and Daoism. However, I do have some things to say about Christian liberal mainline denominations.

I grew up in the United Methodist Church and was a member of the Presbyterian Church (USA) for some twenty years. My experience is that these two liberal denominations continue to see a decline in membership and influence that directly parallels their ongoing acceptance of non-biblical compromises. The words "doctrine," "hell," and "judgment" have become dirty words in most of these denominations, and so they have no difficulty compromising on most any doctrinal aspect of the Bible, especially on the foundational passages from Genesis chapters 1-11. Along with the Episcopal Church, the Evangelical Lutheran Church, and the United Church of Christ, many pastors of the United Methodists and many Presbyterians have joined together to compose the vast majority of those pastors in the United States who have publicly come out in favor of evolution. In my experience, most of the preachers of these two denominations first mentioned seldom use the Bible as the basis for their sermons. Therefore, the sermons they preach are filled with the latest worldly advice and are devoid of any godly meat.

The AAAS position is that all Protestant churches should devolve to the position of these liberal churches concerning the acceptance of evolution and millions of years, which would lead to making the Bible irrelevant for all that do so. Churches of all persuasions struggle to grow and to keep young people in this age of rampant immorality, but the mainline denominations are leading the way to extermination—a situation that I suspect would match the goal of the AAAS.

Buildup toward backlash

"The Fundamentals" listed on page 88 of *The Evolution Dialogues*, no matter who asserted them in the 20th century, are impossible to refute biblically. The higher criticism that brought the "backlash" has been shown to be worthless and invalid by conservative theological scholarship. The truth in the early 20th century was that evolution and millions of years were non-biblical. The truth 100 years later is that evolution and millions of years are non-biblical. Since God and the Bible are the same yesterday, today, tomorrow, and forever, the truth at any time in the future will be that evolution and millions of years are non-biblical. Again we see that acceptance of the AAAS position means rejection of the Bible, and on more than just Genesis 1-11. Anyone, no matter their belief system, could quickly verify that the Bible unequivocally states the truth of the so-called fundamentals. I will not take the time to fill this chapter with the literally hundreds of Scriptures that would attest to that fact.

Evolution on trial

The authors' description of the Scopes Monkey Trial is in large part factual. The 1955 fictional play *Inherit the Wind* was based loosely on the Scopes Trial and had as its stated purpose to take a stand against the McCarthyism of the 1950s. The 1960 movie, however, is much more commonly remembered by the public and was an overt attack on biblical creationism. The movie portrays Bible believing (Southern) Christians as intolerant, ignorant bigots, and totally distorts the facts of the actual Scopes Trial. A very good comparison of the true historical facts to those portrayed in the play and the movie of the Scopes Trial can be found at "The Monkey Trial" website.[19] My personal impression of the play's message and the movie is that "tolerance" is always a good thing and something everyone should strive for, unless it is tolerance of the Biblical Christian worldview and the rights of Biblical Christians to express their opinions in the public marketplace of ideas. "*Inherit the Wind* remains one of the most popular American plays of all time. To this day it remains a favorite production for high schools and colleges and a required-reading book for many school systems."[20]

If one looks into what evolutionary science was being taught in the public schools in Tennessee in 1925, we find that most of it has been determined to be false and abandoned by the evolutionists of today. It is an important fact to note too that the only evolution that was forbidden to be taught in the public schools of Tennessee by the Butler Act was human evolution. A list of some of the major so-called evidences for human evolution that were commonplace in 1925 scientific circles as well as around and at the Scopes Trial follow:

1. *Vestigial Organs:*

At the time of the Scopes Trial many scientists believed that the human body had numerous parts (e.g. tonsils, appendix, little toe, nipples on males, parathyroid gland, thymus, and coccyx) that were vestigial and useless leftovers from man's evolutionary ancestors. Since the 1920s the designed purpose of all these organs has been determined and the vestigial argument has been largely abandoned.[21] Because the purpose of something is not known does not mean it has no purpose. We are currently observing a similar phenomenon with evolutionists' interpretations of DNA. If they don't know the purpose of an aspect of this life-defining molecule they tend to call it "junk."

2. *Embryonic Recapitulation:*

The concept that embryos follow a path of development in the womb that recapitulates the presumed evolution of man from pond scum to fish to amphibian and so forth was popularized by Christian-hating biologist Ernst Haeckel in the 19th century (another contemporary of Lyell and Darwin). Haeckel even faked some of his embryo drawings of humans and animals as "evidence" for his theory. Haeckel's fraud and the falsity of his theory are now well known, but the concept has had a slow death in evolutionary circles and is still touted in some high school biology text books. It seems obvious that one reason for hanging on to this idea is so abortion counselors can try to convince mothers that their unborn babies are just globs of matter. True science has long ago shown that a woman's fertilized egg is a complete human being with a full set of genetic instructions.

The Bible teaches that God takes a personal interest in each person before birth. We read in Psalm 139:13-16, "For you created my inmost being; you knit me together in my mother's womb. I praise you because I am fearfully and wonderfully made; your works are wonderful, I know that full well. My frame was not hidden from you when I was made in the secret place."

3. Neanderthal Man:

At the time of the Scopes Monkey Trial, Neanderthal Man was depicted by scientists as a brute somewhere between an ape and man on the evolutionary time path. The current interpretation of Neanderthal by almost all knowledgeable scientists is he was "completely human. It has been proved that Neanderthals buried their dead, played the flute, organized themselves in social structures, and related to one another as people do today. Neanderthal bones were somewhat more robust that those of modern man, but they still lie within the present range of variation. On average their brains were actually bigger that those of today."[22]

The authors of *The Evolution Dialogues*, on page 144, include an artist's depiction showing Neanderthal (wo)man as a savage. However, using the skeletal evidence, creationist presuppositions, a depiction with modern clothing (including a bra), and a current hairstyle, this gal would not draw any attention as a shopper in the women's section of a typical American department store.

Neanderthal Family Museum Interpretation

One biblical creationist explanation of Neanderthals would be that they were a people forced to migrate away from the Tower of Babel. They would have had language and technology of the time. They ended up migrating to the present day European area, which at that time was very cold, forcing them to survive by living in caves. Neanderthals were not stupid brutes on their way to becoming humans, but were intelligent humans forced to exist in a difficult environmental situation. The human genome has *devolved* since the time of the Neanderthals, thus increasing the effects of mutations. If Neanderthals lived in our times of advanced technology, they might today be among our greatest athletes, scientists, and artists. In fact, it could be said that some of their present day descendants (Europeans) fit that description.

4. Piltdown Man:

A major basis of the ACLU "scientific" case for human evolution in the Scopes case was Piltdown Man "discovered" in 1912 in Piltdown, a small village in England. At the time it was thought by many reputable scientists that fossil evidence consisting of a human skull cap with the jaw of an ape was conclusive proof of ape men having existed. By 1953 it was generally known in the anthropological community that Piltdown Man was a hoax. The human skull cap had been modified to look old and was combined with an ape's jaw where the teeth had been filed down. Nevertheless, as a result of this hoax several generations were influenced to believe in human evolution; and Piltdown man was still in biology textbooks used in classes as evolutionary evidence long after 1953.

The Piltdown Man hoax illustrates the fact that people tend to readily believe things that match their presuppositions no matter what the evidence really shows. As one investigative author put it, "That the gentlemen who launched the Piltdown Man were possessed by the pre-conceived idea that a Missing Link possessing his features would one day be found will become abundantly clear when we observe their pattern of behavior. That the scientific world in general had the same idea was neatly summed up by that famous scientist Sir Arthur Keith in his *Antiquity of Man*, published in 1924: 'That we should discover a race as Piltdown, sooner or later, has been an article of faith in the anthropologist's creed ever since Darwin's time.'"[23]

5. Nebraska Man:

Another "scientific" evidence for the evolution of humans at the time of the Scopes Trial was Nebraska Man. In the June 24, 1922 issue of the *Illustrated London News* a two page story sensationalized the finding of a single tooth found in the state of Nebraska. In the newspaper story an artist was able to illustrate not only the depiction of Nebraska Man but also his slovenly, naked wife as she gathered roots for dinner.

By 1927 it was determined that the tooth was not human, but was instead from the jaw of a pig! This incident is a most spectacular example of how people will believe anything, especially things that advance their presupposed philosophical views.

Nebraska Man and Wife

As each decade goes by new "missing links" are discovered that are given sensational press coverage as being the proof needed to once and for all finally prove the "fact" of evolution. But these proofs are always set aside for the next proof that provides the next missing link that everyone has long awaited. If we only needed one missing link that would prove evolution there would be no need to continue looking for it. In reality, the links are all missing, there are no true transitional fossils, and Darwin's theory is bankrupt and should be buried.

"See to it that no one takes you captive through hollow and deceptive philosophy, which depends on human tradition, and the basic principles of this world rather than on Christ" (Colossians 2:8).

FURTHER READING

1. Bergman, Jerry and Howe, George, *Vestigial Organs Are Fully Functional,* CRS, 1990.
2. Bergman, Jerry, "The Scopes Trial: William J. Bryan's Fight against Eugenics and Racism," *Creation Matters*, Creation Research Society, vol. 15 (1), Jan/Feb. 2010.
3. Cornelius, R.M. and Morris, John D., *Scopes: Creation on Trial,* Master Books, 1999.
4. Desmond, Adrian, *Huxley: From Devil's Disciple to Evolution's High Priest*, Addison-Wesley, 1997.
5. Junker, Reinhard, *Is Man Descended from Adam?* Druckhous Gummersbach, 1998.
6. McDowell, Josh, *The New Evidence That Demands a Verdict,* Thomas Nelson, 1999.

CHAPTER 5
THE SCIENCE BEHIND EVOLUTION

ANGELA'S STORY

"THERE YOU GO again" was a saying used by American President Ronald Reagan in his debates with political opponents. The same quote is quite appropriate for the arguments put forth by evolutionists in chapter 5 of *The Evolution Dialogues*.

Angela explains her father's objections to evolutionary theories to Dr. Dunbar by saying, "My dad says it's one thing to improve a line of cattle through selective breeding, but that cows evolving through other species is impossible." And then she says, "But Dr. Brown also talked about how new species are formed through macroevolution. So my dad was wrong."

Well, there they go again! The authors are playing the evolutionist's favorite game of "confusing definitions" in an attempt to conceal the fact that they have no proof for macroevolution. It is true that evolutionists evidently believe that they "have an overarching explanatory framework that has been carefully constructed." But where is the proof that their theory has been proven by scientific tests? You won't find that proof anywhere in chapter 5. What you will find are statements such as:

1. "Nonetheless, a well-grounded theory does point toward the truth."
2. "…evolution is a theory, one of the greatest of all scientific theories, a theory that provides the most consistent explanation for many known facts."
3. "…nature has been at her job for millennia—macroevolution. Look at this orchid!"

These are statements of faith based on the presuppositions that microevolution can be extrapolated to macroevolution and that the earth is billions of years old. The theory that Dr. Dunbar says "points toward the truth" is grounded on atheistic and deistic presuppositions and nothing more!

In addition, the authors insult the intelligence of their readers when they use the germ theory as an analogy for evolutionary theory. There is plenty of real science that Angela's dad can refer to if he has any doubts about the efficacy of washing his hands to avoid microbe-borne disease. He could study many books and scientific papers that explain the connection of germs to disease. He could even do his own experiments on his farm with the assistance of microscopes and Petri dishes. That would be an example of the valid exercise of the scientific method. There are only comparisons of "apples to oranges" available to evolutionists, and they have nothing else to use.

We learn that the specific "macroevolution" that Dr. Dunbar is selling to Angela on this day is that of orchids. She explained that over long periods of time orchids evolved into orchids and then evolved into more orchids. That is micro-evolutionary change. That is variety within one kind and is not "macroevolution in all of its glory." As Angela's story is paused it seems doubtful that she will be able to convince her father to accept her newfound university learning "because he believes what he believes." But our fictional Dr. Dunbar and the real AAAS believe what they believe too. They believe that given enough time mutations and natural selection will change orchids into something else—perhaps a frog or maybe a prince.

Angela's story continues to be one of atheism versus Christianity. Any Christian who does not realize this will be open to teetering between his Christian faith and a belief in a religion of total inconsistency. Atheists clearly understand this fact as attested by the following quote:

> Christianity has fought, still fights, and will fight science to the desperate end over evolution, because evolution destroys utterly and finally the very reason Jesus' earthly life was supposedly made necessary. Destroy Adam and Eve and the original sin, and in the rubble you will find the sorry remains of the son of god. Take away the meaning of his death. If Jesus was not the redeemer who died for our sins, and this is what evolution means, then Christianity is nothing![24]

THE SCIENCE BEHIND EVOLUTION

What science is

The authors of *The Evolution Dialogues* devote chapter 5 to an attempt at explaining their understanding of what science is and is not. Their opinion can be summarized by four quotes taken from this chapter:

1. "Science is a process through which people seek a better understanding of the natural world around them" (page 98).
2. "Science is the quest for explanations of how things work based on natural processes and structures" (p. 107).
3. "There is a term for a basic principle that undergirds scientific practice. It is methodological naturalism, and it is the assumption that explanations provided by science should make reference only to nature itself" (p. 107).
4. "Science is *not* the only way of knowing. It is a way of knowing based on information attained through human interaction with the natural world" (p. 108).

The authors make a feeble attempt to define their methodological naturalism as not being a philosophical position. That, of course, makes no sense since they admit that their way of determining what makes up science is based on an assumption. This is an assumption that does not allow them to look at evidences except according to their preconceived presuppositions. These are the presuppositions that I have been continuously analyzing and discussing up to this point in *The Creation Dialogues* showing they do in fact have an overt and obvious philosophical position that is not in any way neutral.

This philosophical position forces all evolutionists to commit logical thinking errors that even they admit are not scientific. A good example of this is seen in the explanation for the origin for the long necks of giraffes. On page 99 the authors write, "Explanations that only rely on claims not grounded in the physical world are outside of science." And they add that supernatural explanations are inventions or fables. But previously the authors wrote (p. 98) that, "Through fossil evidence, they [evolutionary scientists] know that the modern giraffe evolved from antelope-like ancestors that lacked an especially long neck." Here again we see how methodological naturalism has forced creation of an invention (fable or fairy tale). The fossil evidence was interpreted only according to their presuppositions. They do not even "know" if the giraffe evolved from anything! No one reported seeing this evolution take place. The fossil evidence consisted of bones, skulls, and teeth of fully formed antelope-like animals and fully formed giraffes. The ancestral connection was simply made in the imaginations of the evolutionists … imaginations that were not and never are grounded in the physical world.

Levels of scientific knowledge

Evolutionists continually draw parallels between valid scientific theories and their evolutionary theories in an attempt to gain respectability for themselves and their theories. The authors admit that, "Each of these theories has unanswered questions at their margins that scientists continue to explore (…What is the pace of evolution?)." But they refuse to address the "elephant in the room" (not a marginal issue at all) which is the question of whether macroevolution has any basis whatsoever in true science.

The construction of knowledge about evolution

Certainty and uncertainty

Many people have different definitions for "science" than do evolutionists with their methodological naturalism. Here is the definition from one common American dictionary:

> sci-ence **n.** [[,L. *scire*, to know]] **1** systemized knowledge derived from observation, study etc. **2** a branch of knowledge, esp. one that systemizes facts, principles and methods **3** skill or technique[25]

Similar definitions are commonly found in most standard American dictionaries. A definition for science often used by creation scientists is:

> Science means "knowledge," not speculative philosophy or naturalism. The essence of the scientific method is measurement, observation, repeatability. The great philosopher of science, Karl Popper, stresses that "falsifiability" is the necessary criterion of genuine science. That is, a hypothesis must—at least in principle—be testable and capable of being refuted, if it is truly scientific.[26]

These definitions are based on the root Latin for the word, showing that science means knowledge. The evolutionists would have Christians ignore or reject the special knowledge that they have access to because of their faith. "in order that they may know the mystery of God, namely, Christ, in whom are hidden all the treasures of wisdom and knowledge" (Colossians 2:2b-3). To accept evolution and millions of years and the evolutionist definition for science, we see that not only does the Bible need to be rejected, but also does God Himself.

There is uncertainty in science, even in creation science, but there is no uncertainty in Christ and the Bible. Christians must never lose sight of this fact when asked by evolutionists (or anyone) to come to a so-called "neutral" position of rejecting the Bible and what it tells us about our Creator God and His creation. Rejecting the Bible is not a neutral position; it is an atheistic position!

Non-scientific interpretations of science

It is my position that naturalism is a wrong worldview, diametrically opposed in every important aspect to the right worldview of Biblical Christianity. Naturalism requires a blind faith and has as its basis a desire to reject the Creator God of the universe. The worldview of naturalism is not, therefore, based on truth as is Biblical Christianity (John 14:6).

When people base their thinking on untruths they will naturally interpret evidences incorrectly and get the wrong answers. This fact is illustrated again in *The Evolution Dialogues* on page 106 where the authors present what they believe are scientific interpretations of geological and biological evidences. They say, "The Earth appears to be 4.6 billion years old, which is long enough for humans to have evolved through natural processes from the first living organisms." With a prevailing definition that science is knowledge rather than speculative philosophy, we can easily see that this statement is not scientific. The earth is presupposed to be 4.6 billion years old and there is no valid scientific evidence that 4.6 billion years would be long enough for human evolution (which itself is also presupposed). This statement is a naturalistic fable not a scientific interpretation.

Similarly they write, "The DNA code is essentially the same for all living organisms on earth due to their common descent from a single ancestor." This too is not a scientific statement but naturalistic philosophy based on the atheistic presuppositions discussed throughout this book. The DNA code is different in some aspect or another for every different lifeform or they would look the same, which they do not. Common sense and biblical interpretations of the homologies involved argue life was engineered by a Common Designer who used a common informational building block of life (DNA) to make various kinds of life that all had to be able to survive on a single planet, earth.

The authors are misinformed or are attempting to mislead when they write that, "Science is also a collective endeavor…They check each other's work, reconfirm or disconfirm observations, and critique each other's analyses" (p. 107). It is my observation that this collectivism is just an idealistic goal that is seldom attained, whether it is good or bad. The driving force behind science is the pursuit of money and the need of the scientists to "publish or perish." In the field of evolution the only real agreement is that evolution is a "fact" with little agreement on any detailed aspect of the so-called fact. The late Dr. Henry Morris published a book in 1997 with literally thousands of secular quotes concerning evolution that strongly document the fact that there is no agreement in secular science on any segment of the macro-evolutionary theories past or present.[27] This should be expected for a theory that is not based on true science. I do not believe that all creation science is true, because creation scientists are as likely to make mistakes as are secularist evolutionists. The only difference is that creation scientists have the big advantage of beginning their science with the Words of God rather than the words of men.

The process of checking each other's scientific work is called replication. Here is what a couple of researchers named Broad and Wade concluded about that process:

Replication is not a normal scientific procedure; it is undertaken only in special circumstances, such as with results of unusual importance or when fraud is suspected on other grounds.[28]

My research of evolutionary scientific articles has confirmed that this is the case, and even some very suspect "science" is seldom replicated, I believe, for two reasons. Firstly, evolutionary science is not real science so there is usually nothing to replicate. Since the conclusions are all presupposed, most of what is written is of a speculative nature and so there is nothing experimental that can be done to determine the truth of the interpretations. As mentioned, how would one scientifically prove what happened in a beginning that cannot be duplicated.

Secondly, in those cases where there is work of an experimental nature, replication is not usually done because only the original researcher gains any fame or remuneration from the work. There is seldom any monetary incentive for someone to redo a work that has been already published. Some of the research I did that led me to come to these conclusions can be found in the work I did on *Archaeopteryx* (see DVD "*Archaeopteryx*: What Was It?"). I found that the secular researchers all started with evolutionary presuppositions and then did their work in an effort to prove their assumptions were correct. Since I had different presuppositions, I came up with different conclusions. I have not made these claims concerning the reasons for no replication with regard to all science…just what is normally identified as evolutionary science. I do not really know that much about the details of operation for the fields of normal secular science, although Broad and Wade indicated that examples of fraud and cheating can be found most anywhere.[29]

In the prologue, I touched on the hysteria prevalent in evolutionary circles these days. I agree with the authors of *The Evolution Dialogues* that every scientist operates with a worldview. But I disagree that personal bias has any way of being balanced out in the current "naturalism only" academic climate for the study of origins evidences. This is because not all of the scientific input is allowed to be considered. Any interpretation at odds with the evolutionary presuppositions is not allowed in the halls or academic publications of those in control (such as AAAS and others like them). The attitude of those who work to exclude creation science is expressed very well by this quote:

Creationists often complain that their theories and their colleagues are discriminated against by educators … As a matter of fact, creationism should be discriminated against … No advocate of such propaganda should be trusted to teach science classes or administer science programs anywhere under any circumstances. Moreover, if any are now doing so, they should be dismissed.…I am glad this kind of discrimination is finally catching on, and I hope the practice becomes much more vigorous and widespread in the future.[30]

And this extreme bias is not exacted exclusively against creationists. Increasingly, anyone who expresses any doubt in Darwinian evolution is subjected to penalties such as degree denial and other career-ending actions. In the book *Slaughter of the Dissidents*,[31] Dr. Jerry Bergman documents what he describes as hate crimes against people (not just creationists) who have serious doubts about the validity of Neo-Darwinism. These "Darwin Doubters" are under continuing attack by the "Darwin fundamentalists" who control academia. Bergman describes many of the current cases where Darwin Doubters are excluded from the table of ideas in academia by the following types of behaviors and actions:

1. Derogatory and Inappropriate Comments
2. Denial of Admittance to Graduate Programs
3. Denial of Degrees
4. Denial of Deserved Promotion
5. Censorship of Darwin-Critical Works from Libraries and Schools
6. Firings, Terminations, and Denial of Tenure
7. Demotions
8. Threats and Personal Intimidation

Dr. Bergman believes that the evidence shows that the situation in academia is much worse than described in the popular movie on the same topic titled, *Expelled—No Intelligence Allowed* with Ben Stein. Eventually the *Slaughter* series is planned to consist of five volumes, each close to 500 pages long with about 1,000 footnotes each!

As a Biblical Christian, I expect that my views will be attacked just as Jesus warned, "If the world hates you, keep in mind that it hated me first" (John 15:18). Peter put it this way, "However, if you suffer as a Christian, do not be ashamed, but praise God that you bear that name" (1 Peter 4:16). But in the United States of America, its citizens are supposed to be protected from the sort of abhorrent discrimination that is being leveled at anyone in academia who disputes the "fact" of macroevolution and millions of years. Today, secular science is not working to exclude bias from its educational system—it is instead working to do the opposite by attempting to establish methodological naturalism as its fundamental and defining religion. The *Expelled* movie showed an evolutionist philosopher of science, Michael Ruse, interviewed, who said he believed life came about "on the backs of crystals." Ruse also wrote, "Evolution is promoted by its practitioners as more than mere science. Evolution is promulgated as an ideology, a secular religion—a full-fledged alternative to Christianity, with meaning and morality.... Evolution is a religion."[32]

Christians must realize that evolution is a replacement for Christ. As a religion, evolution offers no spiritual help, a morality surreptitiously borrowed from Christianity, next to no scientific explanation for life, and absolutely no hope. I realized this in 1984, and my path to the Truth could be described as being somewhat similar to that expressed by another engineer by the name of Henry Morris who wrote:

> The so-called evidences for evolution crumbled away when closely examined and critically ana-lyzed. They certainly were not comparable to the evidence supporting the laws and principles upon which engineers must base their designs. These must be empirically tested and proven before use. The design of a dam or a bridge cannot be based on armchair philosophizing or leap-of-faith extrapolating, as is true of macro-evolutionary theory. On the other hand, the concept of a creator as the explanation of the scientific evidence was eminently satisfying, both intellectually and emotionally, and so I became a creationist.[33]

The effects of evolutionary thinking and indoctrination are not neutral on society either. Some of the more obvious detrimental effects are:

1. In the eyes of many, animals have become equal to humans. This makes sense if we believe that we have evolved from the same common ancestor as animals rather than created in the image of God.
2. Human lives have been devalued to the point that abortion is not a moral issue for many people. This follows from the evolutionary concept that babies in the womb are nothing more than blobs of tissue. About 51 million babies have been aborted in the United States since the *Roe v. Wade* decision. The current American president and his administration have decided that embryonic stem cell research is a worthy pursuit even though it is clear that this is murder in the same sense as is abortion.
3. There is no basis for right and wrong if one believes that evolution is true. Everything is relative then, and since our brains and thoughts are the result of accidents over billions of years, who is to say what is right or wrong?
4. Marriage and family have become redefined to match the ideas of perverse minds rather that the dictates of a loving God. The result is many broken homes, dysfunctional families, and insecure children.
5. Selfishness is becoming a larger problem as people are led to believe that they are a result of random chance events over millions of years. In the minds of many who accept the evolutionary concepts "survival of the fittest" is our creator.

Methodological naturalism is not neutral science, and truth is not to be found in following its dictates. True science follows the correct interpretation of the evidence wherever it leads, even if it leads to the doorstep of a Creator.

"Ah, Sovereign LORD, you have made the heavens and the earth by your great power and outstretched arm. Nothing is too hard for you" (Jeremiah 32:17).

FURTHER READING

1. Bergman, Jerry, *Slaughter of the Dissidents*, Leafcutter Press, 2008.
2. Breese, Dave, *7 Men Who Rule the World From the Grave*, Moody Press, 1990.
3. Broad, William and Wade, Nicholas, *Betrayers of the Truth*, Simon and Schuster, 1982.
4. Morris, Henry, *That Their Words May be Used Against Them*, Master Books, 1997.

CHAPTER 6
CHRISTIAN WORLDVIEWS

THE ANTI-BIBLE BIAS of the authors and sponsors of *The Evolution Dialogues* must be evident to any reader by chapter six, even a casual observer of the origins controversy. It is a bit strange to read a chapter pretending to explain what Christianity is about from such a bias. In chapter six of *The Creation Dialogues,* I hope to correct some of the authors' many errors and omissions concerning the Bible and explain how critical the Bible is to the development of a proper Christian worldview.

ANGELA'S STORY

Angela now indicates that she believes she can "select a trait and create a testable hypothesis for how it may have evolved through natural selection." She has arrived at the point of no return, for if she believes that evolutionists have developed and tested, or can develop and test, hypotheses for macroevolution, her indoctrination into the evolutionist faith is complete.

Her spiritual advisor, Phil, next moves her into considerations of social and psychological evolution and God's place in that evolution. Since Phil does not take the Bible as authoritative on these matters, it should be no surprise that he "doesn't have any answers." And, for Phil to describe God as being a "her" rather than as "Him" is evidence of his total lack of confidence in and respect for God's Word.

Finally, Angela shows that she has total faith in the evolutionary worldview by saying that she believes faith itself is something that has evolved. Biblical Christians do not have perfect knowledge and do not believe they have perfect knowledge, but they do believe that the One who does have perfect knowledge is revealed authoritatively and inerrantly in the Bible. Many Christian students (whether in grade school, high school, or college) who are indoctrinated to believe evolution will eventually lose their faith in God and become "fools." I know that when I was a young person, evolutionary indoctrination had a big effect on me, and by accepting that faith I became a fool. "The fool says in his heart, 'There is no God'" (Psalm 14:1).

CHRISTIAN WORLDVIEWS

Defining Christianity

JAMES OSSUARY

The faith of Christian believers "is not primarily dependent on material evidence." People of all stripes often don't believe material evidence anyway. As Jesus said to the Pharisee Nicodemus, "I have spoken to you of earthly things and you do not believe, how then will you believe if I speak of heavenly things?" (John 3:12).

However, the authors may have jumped the gun when they wrote (p. 114) that the "James ossuary was exposed as a fake." The Israeli forgery trial for the James ossuary (bone box) lasted over four years, involved 75 witnesses and over 9,000 pages of testimony. And the latest on this ossuary as of this writing is as follows:

> In October 2008, after more than three years in court Judge Farkash advised the prosecution to drop the case, which would result in a major embarrassment for the Israeli Antiquities Authority and the Israeli police. The defendants, who have maintained their innocence throughout the ordeal, appear to have been vindicated, along with the *Biblical Archaeological Review*, which among others has consistently supported the authenticity of the inscription [on the ossuary]. That such a discovery would receive much public scrutiny and bias is not unexpected given the political and religious conflicts that surround the historicity of Jesus Christ. Furthermore, human endeavors like archaeology will always be fallible, and authenticating this artifact to the satisfaction of all may not be possible. Nevertheless, the ossuary remains as support for the existence of Jesus and the belief of the 1st-century Church in His resurrection.[34]

Foundations of Christianity

Story (stor̄e) **n.,** *pl.*-**ries** [[<Gr *historia,* narrative]] **1** the telling of an event or events, account; narration, **2** a joke, **3** a fictitious narrative shorter than a novel, **4** the plot of a novel, play, etc., **5** [colloq.] a falsehood, **6** a news report.[35]

The reason I have inserted the above dictionary definitions for the word "story" is because of the different nuances of the word, especially in the present context. For example, when non-believers talk about the "stories" of the Bible they generally mean something other than, "the telling of an event or events, account, narration." In many cases the word "story" is automatically assumed to mean a falsehood, a "joke," or something just made up. Some Bible stories, such as the parables of Jesus, may be hypothetical with the value being in the underlying moral or teaching. Hopefully most Christians have an understanding of this differentiation. The authors of *The Evolution Dialogues* do not place a high historical value on the word (story) when they are writing about the "stories" of the Bible or the "story" of Jesus Christ.

Even many Christians have compromised to the place that the meaning of all biblical stories are to be interpreted in some sort of an allegorical, symbolic, or mythical manner. This sort of compromise is very prevalent with regard to the first eleven chapters of Genesis. These eleven chapters are the ones that bear most directly on the origins issues, which is the subject of the AAAS position and about which this book is focused. The biblical creationist position is Genesis chapters 1-11 are plainly historical narrative, are foundational to the Christian faith, and are not allegory, poetry, or myth. Numerous studies by theological experts have verified that the Genesis accounts are indeed historical narrative. For example, the RATE (Radioisotopes and the Age of the Earth) Group did scholarly statistical analysis research of the original Hebrew language that determined that Genesis 1:1-2:3 is narrative and not poetry.[36]

Most Hebrew scholars agree that the first eleven chapters of Genesis were written to convey the meaning that is plainly there, as evidenced by this quote:

...probably, so far as I know, there is no professor of Hebrew or Old Testament at any world-class university who does not believe that the writer(s) of Genesis 1-11 intended to convey to their readers the ideas that:

(a) creation took place in a series of six days which were the same as the days of 24 hours we now experience,
(b) the figures contained in the Genesis genealogies provided by simple addition a chronology from the beginning of the world up to later stages in the biblical story,
(c) Noah's flood was understood to be world-wide and extinguished all human and animal life except for those in the ark.

Or, to put it negatively, the apologetic arguments which suppose the "days" of creation to be eras of time, the figures of years not to be chronological, and the flood to be a merely local Mesopotamian flood, are not taken seriously by any such professors, as far as I know. The only thing I would say to qualify this is that most such professors may avoid much involvement in that sort of argument and so may not say much explicitly about it one way or the other.[37]

This collection of "stories" that are included in the Bible are very unique in many ways. One way that they are unique is that the collection has one author—God—and one main theme. This theme is the message of salvation through the Lord Jesus Christ. To see this theme one has to take the time and effort to study the Bible, and those who do not study it are not likely to see or understand this theme. The apostle Paul puts it this way, "They are darkened in their understanding and separated from the life of God because of the ignorance that is in them due to the hardening of their hearts" (Ephesians 4:18). Until a person's heart is open to God's Word, the gospel message is blocked to them as Paul wrote, "And even if our gospel is veiled to those who are perishing, the god of this age has blinded the minds of unbelievers, so they cannot see the light of the gospel of the glory of Christ, who is the image of God" (2 Corinthians 4:3-4).

Therefore, it is not surprising that the writers of *The Evolution Dialogues* would leave out so much about the basis for true Christianity. Jesus was *not* a super intelligent homosexual, as Elton John would have you believe. He was *not* just a smart rabbi who told parables and had religious visions. He was and is God! He came into His Creation to be the God-man—the only possible perfect sacrifice for the sins of those who accept Him. While on earth He performed miracles, was crucified, was dead and buried, and was resurrected after three days. He now sits on the right hand of God the Father as judge of all. Evolution or any other of the imaginations of men cannot, and will not, replace Christ, and this fact is the bottom line truth of Christianity. This fact is revealed to us through God's Special Revelation (the Bible) and a perfectly coordinated General Revelation (the Creation).

Christian belief and history

The historicity of Jesus Christ is always an issue with those who want to refute or minimize the Bible. However, the Bible is strongly authenticated by archaeological evidence, and the historicity of Christ is attested to by much secular and Jewish history. Dr. Henry Morris wrote,

Problems still exist, of course, in the complete harmonization of archaeological material with the Bible, but none so serious as not to bear real promise of imminent solution through further investigation. It must be extremely significant that, in view of the great mass of corroborative evidence regarding the biblical history of these periods, there exist today not one unquestionable find of archaeology that proves the Bible to be in error on any point.[38]

Christian apologist Josh McDowell writes concerning Christ's historicity that, "Many ancient secular writers mention Jesus and the movement he birthed. The fact that they are usually antagonistic to Christianity makes them especially good witnesses, since they have nothing to gain by admitting the historicity of the events surrounding a religious leader and His following, which they disdain."[39]

McDowell then proceeds to document evidence from ancient secular writers including the following:

1. Roman historian Cornelius Tacitus (c. A.D. 55-120).
2. Lucian of Samosata, a Greek satirist of the latter half of the second century.
3. Suetonius, who was a Romans historian under Hadrian.
4. Pliny the Younger (A.D. 112) who was the governor of Bithynia in Asia Minor.
5. Thallus, who wrote a history of the Eastern Mediterranean world about A.D. 52.
6. Phlegan, who wrote a history called *Chronicles*, a portion preserved by Julius Africanus.
7. Mara Bar-Serapron, a Syrian and probably Stoic philosopher, wrote of Jesus in a letter to his son after A.D. 70.

It is noteworthy that when the biblical, Jewish (for example Josephus), and extra-Biblical Christian documents are included, more evidence exists for the historicity of Jesus than most (maybe all) other famous people of His time. And, the historicity is almost never questioned by anyone for all of these others. It is an indication of anti-Christian bias to portray the life of Jesus as a "story" as have the authors of *The Evolution Dialogues*. Jesus was, and is, very real.

Even the opponents of Christianity seldom doubted the historicity of Jesus until the 18th and 19th centuries during the time when the ideas of uniformitarianism, millions of years, and organic evolution were conceived and formalized. I doubt that this fact is just a coincidence.

Christians who believe the Bible is God's plainly written and understandable Word have no problem with the historicity of Jesus because of the many assurances actually written in the Bible about that actuality. For example, the apostle John wrote, "Jesus did many other miraculous signs in the presence of his disciples, which are not recorded in this book. But these are written that you may believe that Jesus is the Christ, the Son of God, and that believing you may have life in his name" (John 20:30-31). John also wrote, "Jesus did many other things as well. If every one of them were written down, I suppose that even the whole world would not have room for the books that would be written" (John 21:25). Some may interpret this statement as hyperbole, but I think it is an indication of how many books would be needed to compile all of the information about Christ and His creative acts in the beginning (see John 1:1-3).

Contexts of knowing

The authors of *The Evolution Dialogues* write on page 121, "The focus of religion, its context of knowing, is on what things *mean* rather than on what they *are*." I do not think that claim is true for Biblical Christianity. The point of Jesus' miracles was not just one of His being able to make reality look or act different (unnatural) so as to teach a moral point. No, when the Creator walked on water, turned water into wine, or raised people from the dead, He was demonstrating to all that He was indeed who He said He was. Therefore, He was providing every reason for the witnesses at that time to believe unto martyrdom as well as unto their salvation. The fact that Christianity and the Bible have survived so long is testimony to the success of this initial mode of operation. Christianity is not a religion that is separate from the creation; it is a religion that actually explains the creation, the purposes for it, and God's long term plans for it.

I do not believe that the examples given for different forms of knowledge are relevant to the discussion at hand. The reason for this is that the "science" behind macroevolution is bogus. It is not a correct analogy to infer that the science that explains the boiling of water or the science that explains the biochemistry of nutrition is comparable to the so-called science that evolutionists use to defend their theory in *The Evolution Dialogues*. Biblical creationists have no problem with true science because it is perfectly compatible with the Word of the Creator. Evolution and millions of years are not compatible with either of God's revelations. Evolution and millions of years are contradictory to both of God's revelations. It is time that evolutionists express some humility and cease their attempts to ignore God.

Defining religion

al-tru-ism (al'troo iz' em) **n.** [[<**L** *alter,* other]] unselfish concern for the welfare of others.

Evolutionists conclude that altruism is a result of evolution of mankind in his battle to survive ("survival of the fittest"). People act kindly toward others only in a selfish way since that "enhances survival on the group level" (p. 122). This sort of thinking concerning selfishness matches what the Bible tells us about the sinful nature of humans, "The heart is deceitful above all things and beyond cure. Who can understand it?" (Jeremiah 17:9). The big difference is that the Bible tells us this deceitfulness is a result of turning away from God and not the result of natural selection and millions of years. In the beginning everything was very good and then came the Fall! Christians should, therefore, exhibit altruism not from a position of selfishness but because they are commanded to do so. Jesus said, "Love your neighbor as yourself" (Matthew 22:39). The Old Testament law was provided because mankind had demonstrated that determining right from wrong was not possible without God's help. Paul wrote, "Through the law we became conscious of sin" (Romans 3:20b). Evolutionists have no logical way of determining what is right or wrong and what is moral or immoral if they really believe everything came by accident from nothing. My observation is they have adopted religious morality and then ascribed it to natural selection.

Faith as the starting point

Contested knowledge

The authors admit that all knowledge systems depend on faith of some sort. For Christianity, faith in the teachings of the Bible and faith in Jesus Christ as Lord and Savior are requirements. This is a known aspect of the faith and a stipulation of the promises of our loving God. Accepting the presuppositions of evolution, however, places people into a position where they must have a totally blind faith. Since naturalism requires a natural explanation for all natural events and all events are defined by the faith to be natural, the miracles, the providence, and the possibility of a personal relationship to God are *a priori* ruled out. This then forces evolutionists to believe in spontaneous generation, which science has shown to be impossible. It forces evolutionists to believe in macroevolution when no scientific evidence exists that it has ever occurred or could ever occur. It forces evolutionists to reject all the overwhelming evidence that the earth is young and not billions of years old. And, for most evolutionists, it forces them to reject the Creator God of the universe.

While it is true that the Bible indicates that there is nothing new under the sun (Ecclesiastes 1:9) and that God does not change, it is *not* true that evolutionists are open to changes in their core beliefs from the results of scientific testing. Evolutionary scientists have presuppositions that they are not willing to modify for any reason, and this fact means that the results of their tests will always rule out God and the Bible. This conflict is not one between science and Christianity, but rather between "non-science" (nonsense) and Christianity.

The authors paint the origins controversy as "a controversy between tradition and experience: a tradition that depicts God as Creator intervening in nature's history versus the experience of successful explanations of nature's history without reference to God" (p. 125). Biblical creationists ask "where is the evidence that evolutionary theories have successfully explained nature's history?" And, we are right back to the crux of the issue again. The evidence is presupposed, not proven. The belief system is one of blind faith and not from scientific experimentation. The religion of naturalism is false and truth is not in it!

FURTHER READING

1. Bahnsen, Greg L., *Always Ready*, Bahnsen, 1996.
2. Lisle, Jason, *Ultimate Proof of Creation*, Master Books, 2009.
3. McDowell, Josh, *The New Evidence That Demands a Verdict*, Thomas Nelson Publishers, 1999.
4. Morris, Henry, *Biblical Creationism*, Master Books, 2000.
5. Pearcey, Nancy R. and Thaxton, Charles B., *The Soul of Science*, Crossway Books, 1994.

CHAPTER 7

THE WORLD AS EXPLAINED BY EVOLUTION

ANGELA'S STORY

ONE OF THE biggest challenges I had when I was an evolutionist was explaining to myself or others the meaning of life in general. Related was the similar problem of understanding my own purpose in the world. While naturalism was obviously presented to me as the best way to understand the universe, it became more and more unsatisfactory as a viable worldview as I got older. This was because whenever a truly important, mysterious or difficult question was raised, naturalism had to defer to another realm. Many times these other realms were called, even by naturalists, the supernatural or God or gods, and this practice became even more confusing to me because the philosophy (or religion) of naturalism was promoted as a "scientific" method for explaining everything without a need for God. As an evolutionist I couldn't figure out if naturalism really had reliable answers for any of the really big questions of life.

In chapter 7 of *The Evolution Dialogues,* Angela has reached that point of inquiry in her life as well. Evolutionists are great at describing their theories of "everything from nothing for no ultimate reason," but will often then make conversation about the soul, God's reflection, God's image, and other non-secular topics that indicate that they don't even really believe the most basic fundamentals of their own faith. This type of behavior is demonstrated in the hypothetical conversation between Angela and Dr. Dunbar. It seems that evolutionists are just humoring the Christian with such conversations. Whether they are sincere or not, this inconsistency is what, for the most part, drove me finally to Jesus Christ and away from the fairy tales of naturalism.

Twenty years after my acceptance of Christ as my Lord and Savior and my conversion to creationism, I purposed to develop a ministry through which I could explain to others what I had learned about the meaning and purpose of life. By 2004 I had begun my speaking and writing ministry *Creation Engineering Concepts*, had founded The Institute for Creation Science, and had settled on the following principles of my ministry:

1. **Worldview & Truth**: Biblical Christianity is the only worldview that provides a consistent explanation of all the facts of reality with regard to origins, theology, philosophy, ethics, economics, or anything else. This worldview is relevant to all of life because it is based on truth. It is the only worldview based on truth, a truth that is grounded in Divine Revelation.

2. **Biblical Creation Apologetics & Truth:** The purpose and methodology of Biblical Creation Apologetics is to attempt to explain reality using the bases of God's Special Revelation (The Bible) and God's General Revelation (His Creation). The proper investigation of God's revelations is the true science that results in a defense of the Christian faith as well as the clearest possible understanding of the history of the universe. Methodological Naturalism is a false science that rejects God's Special Revelation, often misinterprets God's General Revelation, and provides an incorrect history of the universe.

3. **Genesis Chapters 1-11 & Truth:** A careful and thorough examination of the true history of the universe indicates that a literal acceptance of Genesis chapters 1-11 is foundational to the Gospel message of the Bible and to Christianity itself, and cannot be deleted or compromised if the total God-revealed truth is to be known and understood.

4. **Origins & Truth:** There are only two possible explanations for the origin of all things. Either the universe was created from nothing by the will of God in a supernatural way as described in the Bible, or it was self-created from nothing according to the constantly changing theories of men. Either life was created by God, each type according to its kind as explained in the Bible, or it has evolved by chance over millions of years from an original state of nothingness.

5. **Faith & Truth:** Since the origin of all things occurred in the past and the origin mechanisms cannot be duplicated by men in the laboratory, truth regarding origins must be accepted on faith. One must choose between the faith based on the Word provided to man by the infallible Creator God who was there at the beginning, and a blind faith based on naturalistic, God-rejecting, and constantly changing, evolutionary theories of fallible men.

Columbia Gorge from Oregon Side

Until, and unless, our hypothetical Angela realizes that her acceptance of evolution as a basis for her worldview will preclude her from understanding reality as it is instead of how it is not, she will never be able to come to the Truth.

The World as Explained by Evolution

Diversity beyond Measure

I have found evolutionists have only a few types of arguments that they use to defend their faith. Each of these arguments rests on the presuppositions introduced in the prologue. I determined these presuppositions by years of study of secular paleontology articles and books, but I believe they hold perfectly for evolutionary biology, anthropology, and geology as well:

1. There is no God or God is irrelevant.
2. Everything came from nothing.
3. All lifeforms evolved from common ancestors over billions of years.
4. Homology (the study of similar characteristics) alone proves the evolution of all extinct and living lifeforms.

Not all evolutionists agree that these are foundational worldview presuppositions, but I submit that they are whether they realize it or not.

EVOLUTIONIST ARGUMENT TYPES

Experts on many topics have a tendency to support their ways of thinking by saying that it is true because it is "just so." This "just so" mentality is found in many fields of expertise, but is particularly pervasive in areas normally defined as religious. As a Christian I admit that it is often found in the formal and informal discussions of Christians concerning the Bible. However, evolutionists are, in my opinion, masters of the "just so" argument. This points to two important truths about evolution:

1. It is a religion.
2. It is not science (knowledge).

Therefore, those who want to evaluate the claims of methodological naturalism must develop an awareness of this evolutionist tactic that is intentionally used in an attempt to "snow" people into thinking that science supports their way of thinking. Biblical creationists know that their own hope is faith based, but the fact that Christianity and the Bible are strongly supported historically as well as logically gives them confidence to trust the science based on that faith. Our presuppositions are common sense corollaries to our faith, which itself is consistent with reality.

Evolutionists use "just so" arguments, and you must believe them because they are the ones wearing the lab coats and say their arguments are truth. But, an even better breakdown of evolutionist arguments may be the following three categories:

- Interpretation Stated as Fact (ISF)
- Since microevolution has been demonstrated, then macroevolution is proven (Mi>>Ma)
- Any biological fact, observation, experiment, or hypothesis in and of itself proves evolution (Bi=Ev)

In my study of evolutionist arguments, I have been able to place all of them within one or more of these three categories. Many of the evolutionist arguments are also "just so" but I would like to proceed from this point using just these three categories. Remember too that for evolutionists the word *science* is defined as "methodological naturalism" not "knowledge."

For *The Evolution Dialogues* I conducted an additional read with the sole purpose of categorizing all of the arguments for evolution and millions of years that were provided in the book. The following results are a fairly accurate representation of the arguments:

ISF Arguments = 104
Mi>>Ma Arguments = 26
Bi = Ev Arguments = 8
Total Arguments = 138

I first discussed the ISF argument in the prologue of *The Creation Dialogues*. I said then that much of the information of evolutionists is presented as fact when it is not, but rather is interpretation based on evolutionary philosophical presuppositions. My compilation of arguments resulted in the ISF argument being used about 75% of the time in the book. Chapter 7 of *The Evolution Dialogues* is filled with the ISF argument type, as I counted at least 50 instances in that chapter alone. One who is not aware of what is going on here could easily be duped into thinking that the evidence for evolution is overwhelming.

But, using biblical creationist presuppositions the resulting "facts" (interpretations) would be entirely and consistently different for each and every one of these topics.

For many Christians, God is understood to be omnipotent, omniscient, and omnipresent—an awesome yet personal God. On the other hand, methodological naturalism does not allow for prayer, miracles, providence, the resurrection, life everlasting, or a personal relationship with any supernatural entity. Christians must understand this when they are considering whether or not to accept any of the presuppositions of the evolutionists. The Christian God of the Bible is certainly big enough to provide "diversity beyond measure," and the creation scientist understands that God created much diversity within life kinds in the beginning as well as engineering the capability for rapid additional variability into all of life at the same time. This designed adaptability is what allows lifeforms to adapt to changing environmental and ecological conditions. The fact that science has found that life can rapidly adapt to its environment is a stronger argument for creation 6,000 years ago than for evolution over millions of years.

One Big Family

There is absolutely no question that the Bible portrays God as a personal God. What would be the point of asking our God into our hearts and lives if He does not exist or if He only set things into motion billions of years ago to play out in some way via mutations and natural selection? Besides the doctrinal truth of sin leading to death (first discussed in the prologue), the doctrine of Christ's death and resurrection is absolutely critical to Biblical Christianity. As Paul wrote in 1 Corinthians 15:13-14, "If there is no resurrection of the dead, then not even Christ has been raised. And if Christ has not been raised, our preaching is useless and so is your faith." Those who call themselves Christians and do not believe in the resurrection are, as Paul put it, "to be pitied more than all men" (1 Corinthians 15:19). These two doctrines in themselves have no way of being logically incorporated into the evolutionist's belief that, "all species stem from a common ancestor, and this is what explains the likeness in the DNA of distinct species."

This evolutionist DNA argument is another ISF and is easily offset by the biblical view that the complexity and design in life is due to the engineering expertise of our awesome Creative Designer, not evolution over eons from a common ancestor!

The fact that the DNA sequence is remarkably similar between species can be interpreted to mean that the Creator chose to use the same DNA "building blocks and codes" for numerous resulting creatures. It does not have to mean everything came from the same common ancestor. The function desired and the material available is what determines how the (intelligent) engineer uses his applied science, experience, and art to come up with something that works to solve a problem. All engineers know for sure that nothing is what comes from nothing and that nothing (outside of life) can build itself. Creationist Paul Abramson has been known to use the illustration of visualizing an empty cardboard box up in the attic to be checked on periodically to see if the big bang or spontaneous generation has produced anything inside of it. We all know what the results of such an experiment would be—nothing. Intelligence is always required to provide information, and information is obviously what DNA was designed to provide.

This argument does not require a PhD in any field of evolutionary science. Here is another common sense argument from another source:

> If human *similarity* to apes is evidence that an apelike creature evolved into man, why aren't the *vast differences* between man and ape accepted as evidences that man did *not* descend from apes? The human nose is totally different from that of primates; man's lips are formed differently; apes have thumbs on their feet, while men do not; man's head is located at a different position on the spinal column; and human babies are far more dependent upon their mothers at birth than apes.
>
> Even more physically perplexing is the fact that apes have a bone in the male's reproductive organ, while the human male makes use of an incredibly complicated hydraulic system. How could anyone reasonably conclude that the bone in an ape's reproductive organ slowly evolved into mankind's complex hormonal/hydraulic mechanism by some step-at-time mutational process? If the bone disappeared before the human system was completely in place, the apelike creature would not be able to reproduce and survive. Since apes have no difficulty reproducing, why would the human hydraulic system have ever evolved?
>
> Dr. John C. Whitcomb observed that '*While the physical differences between man and primate are quite great, the spiritual/linguistic/cultural differences are little short of infinite.*' It is extremely poor and superficial science to conclude that some apelike creature evolved into mankind.[40]

And I would add that visualizing that the change from an ape penis to a human penis occurred quickly (as in the theory of punctuated equilibrium) is even more fantastic as well as "perplexing" beyond belief.

Christians must never lose sight of the fact that evolutionists believe that homology is the main thing they think they need to prove common ancestry. And the similarities in structure (or DNA) prove to them that everything came from a common ancestor way back when. But the existence of a competing biblical creationist Common Designer hypothesis proves that the evolutionary belief is only a presupposition. If evolutionists have a time machine that allows them to go back in time to observe the macro-evolutionary changes that supposedly took place, why can't they fill in any of the blanks for the common ancestors on their phylogenetic diagrams? They don't have a time machine and so all of the common ancestors must be presupposed. The Bible tells us that there were "kinds" in the beginning and so Christian believers can know that the evolutionary hypothesis is just that (a hypothesis) and not a valid theory.

Life's Origins

The fact that evolutionists have no idea how life originated is supported by all of the "probablys" they insert in their beginning of life stories. However, their presuppositions require that they continue to have faith that it must have happened. Somehow life popped out of a rock or crawled out of some ooze. The following quote captures the mindset perfectly: "One has only to contemplate the magnitude of this task to concede that the spontaneous generation of a living organism is impossible. Yet here we are—as a result, I believe, of spontaneous generation."[41]

A more current statement of the situation is: "More than 30 years of experimentation on the origin of life in the fields of chemical and molecular evolution have led to a better perception of the immensity of the problem of the origin of life on Earth rather than to its solution. At present all discussions or principal theories and experiments in the field either end in stalemate or in a confession of ignorance."[42]

As a junior high school student I was the first kid in my school to stay up and visually see the first Sputnik satellite. I also was the only person in my high school I knew of who had a reflector telescope. So, I developed an interest in astronomy and space travel at an early age. Throughout college I paid for a subscription to *Aviation Week & Space Technology* magazine while my fellow students were subscribing to *Time, Sports Illustrated,* and *Playboy.* Among the things that I eventually learned from my interest in astronomy and space travel were the following:

1. The Solar System looks to be young—much younger than the generally reported 4.6 billion years. There is substantial evidence available that can be interpreted so that the Solar System is less than 10,000 years old.

2. The universe is so vast that most of what is written about it outside of our solar system is total conjecture. I tend to trust the evidences reported by scientists regarding the solar system because we have been there or we have sent robots there to gather the information. I generally do not trust the evidences speculated about the rest of the universe since it is based almost entirely on indirect information and philosophy.

Unique Planets of Our Solar System

3. Scientists who say they are Christians and believe in the origin of everything as the result of a big bang are first and foremost believers in big bang theory and only secondarily believers in Jesus Christ. That is, it is my observation that the big bang is number one in their lives and Christ is further on down the list. Most of these scientists are most likely not Christians at all, but rather deists or Unitarians just as were so many of those in the 19th century who got the Western World off on this God-minimizing tangent in the first place.

As I read the evolutionary explanations for the origin of the universe I am reminded of the classic story *Alice in Wonderland*. Mankind does have a tremendous imaginative capability, which is a good thing. But mankind also can and does have the capability to believe anything, including the fairy tales of evolution, as I have stated before.

Nevertheless, as I look at the evidence from deep space I notice two very significant things. First, there looks to be about the same number of galaxies in every direction we look from the earth. This could indicate that our galaxy and thus the earth is located at the center of the universe, which is exactly opposite from the assumptions behind the big bang theory, which requires that the earth be located randomly in an infinite space. Also, it has recently been discovered that the galaxies seem to be spread out from the Milky Way in defined concentric spheres. Again, this is evidence that the earth probably is at the center of everything. Perhaps God really did and does focus on mankind in His creation just as the Bible tells us. In Psalm 104:2 we read, "he stretches out the heavens like a tent..." and this may provide us with some information that could explain how the universe really was created—a theory based on God's truth rather than on the atheistic concept of everything from nothing for no reason in a big bang. Thankfully, there are indeed a number of creation scientists who have been and are working on theories that would scientifically explain the creation, condition, and extent of the universe from a biblical worldview. Science could use many more investigators with open minds like these men.

"The day is yours and yours also the night; you established the sun and moon. It was you who set all the boundaries of the earth; you made both summer and winter. Rise up, O God, and defend your cause; remember how fools mock you all day long. Do not ignore the clamor of your adversaries, the uproar of your enemies which rises continually" (Psalm 74:16-17 and 22-23).

FURTHER READING

1. Baugh, Carl, *Why Do Men Believe Evolution against All Odds?* Hearthstone Publishing, 1999.
2. Behe, Michael J., *Darwin's Black Box*, The Free Press, 1996.
3. Sanford, John, *Genetic Entropy & the Mystery of the Genome*, Ivan Press, 2005.

CHAPTER 8
WHAT IS IN THE MUSEUMS?

UP TO THIS point in *The Creation Dialogues* I have been commenting mostly on the shortcomings of the naturalistic viewpoint and the fact that it cannot in any way be logically received into the Biblical Christian worldview. It is now time for me to report some of the findings from my personal creationist field research on the matter of origins. Over the past decade I have conducted a number of field trips to investigate the evidence. These investigations can be categorized into the two broad categories of "Museums" and "The Field." In this chapter I will concentrate on the museum evidence. You should not be surprised that my findings from both the museums and the field evidences consistently were at odds with the evolutionary worldview. The museum investigations are as follows:

1. Carnegie Museum of Natural History, Pittsburg, PA
2. The La Brea Tar Pits, Los Angeles, CA
3. Smithsonian Natural History Museum, Washington, DC
4. Museum of the Rockies, Bozeman, MT
5. BYU Earth Science Museum, Provo, UT
6. The Prehistoric Museum, Price, UT

As the reader should understand by now, the presuppositions that will be in place during the reporting of my findings will be those listed earlier for the biblical creation scientist and are:

- In the beginning God created everything.
- The Bible is God's true word to mankind.

- God created in six ordinary days only thousands of years ago.
- A worldwide flood destroyed all land animals and humans, except for those on Noah's Ark some 4,500 years ago.

CARNEGIE MUSEUM OF NATURAL HISTORY

Industrialist Andrew Carnegie established the Carnegie Museum in 1895. "Robber Baron" Carnegie's bent toward social Darwinism fit well with his passion to collect dinosaurs and other fossils. Many of the Carnegie museum skeletons on display are the result of the early competition with other museums in the late 19th and early 20th centuries: a race to collect the most and the newest of (especially) dinosaur fossils from mostly the western states of the United States.

At the Carnegie Museum I found that most of the dinosaur skeletons on display were assembled from numerous individual specimens. This is a fact that is not always made evident in the displays. Also I found that the skull of the *Diplodocus carnegi* (the first dinosaur displayed at Carnegie museum) was smashed flat when it was found in the Morrison Formation of Wyoming. In fact the skull in the displayed skeleton is modeled after two partial skulls. In addition, parts from five other Sauropod types of dinosaurs were incorporated into the mounted *Diplodocus*.[43]

Subsequent study of numerous dinosaur fossil sites confirms that vertebrate fossils are usually found in a condition of disarticulation where the bones are ripped apart and spread over areas in the sedimentary layers where they are found. This is why there is always a considerable amount of doubt possible when looking at a mounted skeleton in a natural history museum. Does the skeleton actually represent reality?

More importantly the condition in which the skulls, bones, teeth, and claws are found matches what we would expect if there really was a cataclysmic worldwide Flood as described in the Bible. Evolutionists know that a requirement for fossilization is the rapid and complete burial of an organism. Yet, the explanations given for the fossilization as shown in most museums and books nearly always depict the animal dying or coming to rest in a sandbank next to a relatively slow moving lake or river.

Therefore, I have concluded that the condition in which fossils (vertebrate especially) are found screams catastrophe, and this is what we would expect if there really was a fairly recent worldwide flood.

LA BREA TAR PITS

Rancho La Brea, in Hancock Park located in Los Angeles, California, is one of the richest and most famous asphalt deposits of fossils in the world. Since 1909, more than one million fossil bones have been recovered and housed at the Page Museum at the La Brea Tar Pits. The Page Museum officially estimates that fossil bones representing 231 species of vertebrates, 159 kinds of plants, and 234 kinds of invertebrates have been identified. Some of the larger mammals that are represented in the Page Museum collections include: Sabertoothed cat *(Smilodon)*, Dire wolf *(Canis dirus)*, Giant ground sloth *(Paramylodon)*, Ancient bison *(Bison antiquus)*, Western horse *(Equus occidentalis)*, Western camel *(Camelops hesternus)*, Stilt legged llama *(Hemiauchenia)*, Columbian

The Page Museum at La Brea Tar Pits

mammoth *(Mammuthus columbi)*, Giant short-faced bear *(Arctodus simus)*, Black bear *(Ursus americanus)*, Grizzly bear *(Ursus arctos)*, and Timber wolf *(Canis lupus)*.

The extinct Dire wolves are the most common large mammals from La Brea, with several thousand individuals represented in the Page Museum collections. In the La Brea Museum there are displayed 404 upper skull sections of the Dire wolf, all of which were recovered from the tar pits. The remains of over 2,000 individuals of the state fossil for California, *Smilodon* or sabertoothed cat rank second. If you were to go to the internet website of the Page Museum at ***www.tarpits.org***, you would read the official explanation for the accumulation of these fossils as follows:

Smilodon or Sabertoothed Cat Reconstruction

Asphalt is very sticky, particularly when it is warm. The warm temperatures from late spring to early fall would have provided the optimum conditions for entrapment in asphalt. Small mammals, birds and insects inadvertently coming into contact with it would be immobilized as if they were trapped in flypaper. The feet and legs of heavier animals might sink two or three inches below the surface. Depending on the time of day or year, strong and healthy animals may have managed to escape, but others would have been held fast until they died of exhaustion, or fell prey to passing predators. Under the right conditions, a single mired large herbivore would attract the attention of a dozen or more hungry carnivorous birds and mammals, some of which would find themselves trapped, providing food for other carnivores.

This cycle repeated during the 30,000 years that fossils were accumulating at Rancho La Brea. It is estimated that one entrapment episode involving ten large mammals every decade would furnish more than enough fossil remains to account for all the large mammal and bird fossils collected since the turn of the 20th century (over 1 million!).

So, that is the official explanation. It of course is designed to match uniformitarian geological and biological presuppositions of evolution and millions of years. Since it is the official theory it is widely accepted by scientists and the public, although the entrapment theory has failed to give convincing answers to some key evidentiary questions, which are indicated by the following observations:

1. The physical characteristics of the pits do not seem to allow large entrapment episodes.
2. The tremendous fragmentation and chaotic intermingling of the bones into bone jumbles does not indicate entrapment.
3. The numerical preponderance of carnivores does not match the conditions of the natural world.

Mr. William Weston of Anaheim, California, became a Christian in December of 1972. He holds to the literal inspiration of the Bible, believing the world was created 6,000 years ago and the Genesis Flood occurred about 4,500 years ago. He has been studying the fossils of La Brea since about 2001. He began his study of the La Brea fossils after he read in Whitcomb and Morris's book, *The Genesis Flood* that the La Brea Tar Pits may be a Flood deposition site. Due to the proximity of this fossil site to his home in Anaheim, he decided to do some research. Through the kindness of a non-Christian museum staff member, he was given access to the field notes of the original tar pit excavations. Over time, Mr. Weston gained more privileges regarding the fossil collection and was allowed to do hands on research as an official museum researcher.

Through this research Mr. Weston discovered evidence challenging the traditional entrapment theory and supporting a catastrophic flood theory. As I have visited the La Brea Tar Pits, I have found it enlightening to look at them through the interpretations provided by the research of Mr. Weston. Mr. Weston says, "I have done numerous lectures on the La Brea Tar Pits around Southern California, and have led museum tours for homeschool and Christian school groups. My goal is to present the bare facts of the La Brea Tar Pits, and to provide an interpretation that best explains the facts, meaning the Genesis Flood."[44]

Now, if you visit the La Brea Tar Pits at Hancock Park you will see some tar seeps forming puddles up to 4 feet in diameter. If on a slope, the seep can spread farther, perhaps as much as 15 feet or more. When I have visited Hancock Park, I have seen some of these seeps and I have thought that it was interesting that some were out in the open and unfenced. There is a water-filled lake on the site that is the result of asphalt mining in the early 20th century and that is completely fenced. So, I would rate the hazards to life and limb at Hancock Park in the following order of declining danger:

1. Getting hit by a car in the parking lot.
2. Falling down the stairs of one of the museums on site.
3. Getting mugged by a criminal.
4. Drowning in Hancock Park Lake.

And last and least,

5. Getting stuck in a tar seep.

So, we have heard the official theory for the fossils before. The death trap theory, which was first hypothesized in 1906, says that animals were trapped in the tar, and then numerous carnivores came running and got trapped as well. Here is Bill Weston's summary statement regarding the official theory and any theory that proposes large animal entrapment in tar:

"Although generally accepted by the scientific establishment, there are no observational or experimental data that show that tar puddles have the viscosity to capture large animals, including such mega fauna as elephants and bison. Even local anecdotes about horses and cows standing trapped in tar puddles, whether true or not, cannot properly be called scientific proof if they lack such routine items of information as time, place, and names of witnesses. Considering the lack of solid evidence, the tar puddle theory does not merit further discussion."

Earlier I spoke of the major anomalies of the Tar Pits that tend to discredit the entrapment theory. The first one was the physical characteristics of the tar pits. In summary, what this means is that the shapes of many of the pits that the fossil bones are found in do not lend themselves to trapping numerous large animals. For example, tar pit 16 was only four feet wide with vertical sides. Pit 16 then went down from the top 21 feet before it tapered three more feet to a three-inch wide chimney—the opening through which the asphalt entered from deeper in the earth's crust. Bones from numerous Dire wolves, sabertoothed cats, coyotes, camels, bison, horses, and even a bulky mastodon had been found in pit 16 during the period 1905 to 1915. It is difficult to

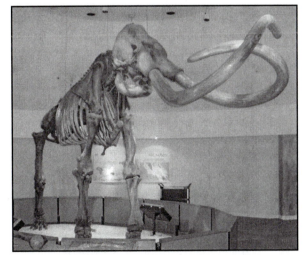

Columbian Mammoth at Page Museum

imagine how all of these large animals managed to squeeze into a hole not much wider than a bathtub.

It is interesting to note that the County of Los Angeles dug 96 test holes in 1913 in order to find pits with fossils in them. Of these 96 test holes only 16 turned up pits with significant quantities of bones. By 1915 all of these pits had been emptied of their bones, the bones were packed in wooden crates and placed in storage. Pit 91 was partially excavated and then reburied.

Then in 1969, pit 91 was reactivated and methodical excavations continued for many more years. This more meticulous identification of position, type, and orientation of fossils (and not just fossil bones, but all types of fossils) has contributed a wealth of detailed scientific information that was previously unknown. This new information has not been kind toward the entrapment theory but has been helpful for creationist theory. At about six feet below the surface of the ground was found an ancient streambed that ran from east to west and curved toward the south wall. Also found were layers of sediment, which would indicate that moving water contributed to formation of the contents of pit 91.

The next great question is why there is such a tremendous amount of bone fragmentation and chaotic bone intermingling. Mr. Weston's description of more recent pit findings as written in his March 2002 paper shed some light on this:

> As excavators removed the contents of these four pits, they noticed that the tar had preserved the bones to a remarkable degree. Even such delicate features as the courses for nerves and blood vessels were discernable. Also found were various kinds of insects in all their minute detail, including wings and antennae…. The superior grade of preservation that characterized the individual specimens stood in stark contrast to the ravaged appearance of the fossil material as a whole. A majority of the bones were damaged in some way: sharp-edged broken ends, splinters, cracks, impact depressions, deep grooves, broken-off chips, and/or heavy abrasions…. In addition, the bones were in an entangled mass, closely pressed together, and interlocked in all possible ways. After separating out the bones, scientists could only guess how the parts of individual animals matched up to one another. They also came to realize that the pits were missing a lot of skeletal parts that they had originally expected to find.[45]

Doesn't this sound a lot like some huge water catastrophe had overtaken these creatures whose bones were found in the tar pits? However logical this conclusion might be, it was, is, and will be unacceptable to those who are totally committed to the uniformitarian philosophy. Thus we have the continued investment by so many in the tar entrapment theory.

The third big mystery that continues to baffle uniformitarian scientists is the numerical preponderance of carnivores in the tar pits. Whereas wolf-to-deer populations in Canada and the United States show a ratio of 100 to 150 herbivores for every carnivore, the La Brea Tar Pits ratio is inverse to that. In other words, the La Brea findings showed that carnivores represent 85% of the total number of individual animals. In addition, flesh-eating birds are about 70% of the total number of birds. The question is why would an eagle, for example, be more vulnerable to entrapment compared to pigeons and doves?

The best explanation that Uniformitarians can come up with is as follows:

> For every large herbivore in the collections there is a saber tooth, a coyote, and four dire wolves. These proportions, so unlike those of natural communities, suggest that the carnivores became selectively trapped when feeding from herbivores that fell victim to the seeps. The large number of flesh eating birds has been explained similarly.[46]

Mr. Weston reports that some scientific evidence does not support this explanation. In 1934, a wildlife specialist in Grand Canyon National Park noticed that birds were getting caught in a tar pit that had been left over from a road construction project several years previously. The wildlife specialist, Mr. A.E. Borell, found bird carcasses in all stages of decomposition from skeletons to those that had just recently died. Mr. Borell found that the contents of the pit consisted of 123 individual birds of 13 different species. Six of these birds were hawks. Thirty days later a repeat visit found eight more dead birds in the pit, none of which were hawks. This ratio of 131 herbivores to six carnivores reflects the expected balance in nature, and is inverse to the ratio found at Rancho La Brea.

Thus many of the individual tar pits were not of the proper size or shape to have captured so many large animals. Furthermore the bone jumbles of the tar pits do not indicate that individual animals were trapped in tar, and a preponderance of carnivores does not make sense in the tar entrapment theory.

Other anomalies that indicate the entrapment theory is incorrect and some sort of catastrophic pre-event is a more likely explanation for what is found at the tar pits include:

1. The lack of teeth marks on herbivore bones.
2. The total lack of soft tissues in the fossils.

Harlan's Ground Sloth at Page Museum

3. The numerical superiority of water beetles among insect species.
4. Water saturation of wood debris found in the pits.

These additional anomalous evidences point away from animal entrapment and toward some sort of a catastrophic diluvial event for several reasons. First consider the lack of teeth marks on herbivore bones found in the tar pits. Remember that La Brea (and there are similar fossil sites in Peru and in France) has a preponderance of carnivore fossils. If these fossil sites were locations of feeding frenzies there should be all manner of teeth marks on the herbivore bones found—but there are few, if any. A catastrophic theory put forward in 1894 by English geologist Joseph Prestwich from the evidence at the site in France makes some very logical sense. According to Mr. Prestwich, a gigantic local flood submerged Western Europe. Prestwich theorized that the flood would naturally drive the animals in the plains to search for higher ground. Frantically fleeing in terror and cowed by the common danger, carnivores and herbivores alike sought refuge in some of the higher areas, and together suffered the same fate whenever the hill was isolated and not high enough to allow escape from the on-rushing flood. Prestwich hypothesized that the dead animals would form a mat on the surface of the water, and eventually body parts detached and fell irregularly onto the submerged surfaces below.

This theory would also explain the preponderance of wolf bones since wolves are generally stronger, more resourceful, and more socially organized than other animals. They would therefore be among the last to be overtaken.

This type of thinking also coincides with the creationist interpretation of the geologic rock record in general. For example, in their book the *Genesis Flood* in 1961, Whitcomb and Morris explained the depth of various fossil remains as due to generally ecological causes. Higher levels of fossils in the earth's strata would be due to the following reasons:

1. Animals of increasing mobility would have increasing ability to postpone inundation.
2. Animals of increasing elevation of habitat would have more time before the rising flood would attain stages sufficient to overtake and cover them.

Next, consider the effects of tar and water on the fossil remains that have been discovered in these tar pits. A large portion of Mr. Weston's research had to do with these effects. What he found in a nutshell are the following:

A. Petroleum or oil tends to act as a preservative for fossils, perhaps for thousands of years.
B. Water tends to act to facilitate the decomposition and desiccation of insect and other animal bodies.

The fact that there is no soft tissue on the fossil bones at La Brea, even though they are encased in a preservative, very likely indicates that there has been definite water action on the bones and insect bodies. The fact that there is a preponderance of water beetle fossils in the pits also would seem to indicate that water may have been a large factor in the accumulation of these fossils. Mr. Weston summarizes this by saying:

> The high concentration of water beetles and water fowl at Pleistocene fossil sites [like La Brea and the other sites we have been discussing] may be an effect of the Genesis Flood. As creatures moved toward higher ground in their efforts to survive, the ones that could swim or float would have had an advantage over the strictly terrestrial types. The species living in the mountains would have had an advantage over the ones living on the plain ... Eventually the Flood overwhelmed them all, but those that survived longer into the Flood period would be buried in the upper, or Pleistocene, levels of sedimentation while the ones that died earlier would be scattered in the lower strata.[47]

Therefore, we can see from the evidence that the Genesis Flood was a source of disarticulated bones that eventually were transported and redistributed to lower elevations by post-Flood fluvial activity. Bones may have traveled hundreds of miles or more from the original habitat of the living animals to their final resting places on the plains. Some bones and soggy wood debris entered a small number of funnel shaped pits, newly formed by natural gas blowouts caused by earthquake tremors. Oil from ruptured underground reservoirs seeped into these pits and flowed over the surrounding bone-strewn plain. This lake of oil thickened into tar, and its surface developed a hard crust, which sealed the pits and kept the matrix in a semi liquid state.

Because of my visits to the La Brea Tar Pits and the valuable work of Mr. Weston, it has become clear to me that this hypothesis provides tremendous explanatory advantages over the official entrapment theory. Therefore, I would conclude that the fossils of the La Brea Tar Pits are most likely an immediate or secondary result of the Genesis Flood some 4500 years ago and the La Brea Tar Pits are definitely not the "Death Trap of the Ages."

SMITHSONIAN NATURAL HISTORY MUSEUM

At the Smithsonian can be found many fossils of animals extinct and still living, all of which are displayed based upon the usual evolutionary and uniformitarian presuppositions discussed throughout *The Creation Dialogues*. The anti-Christian bias is overt, with one indicator being the fact that the museum signs that indicate the time before Christ use the B.C.E. (Before Common Era) notation instead of the standard B.C. (Before Christ) that most people in the western world are familiar with.

B.C.E. means "Before Common Era"

As one looks at the many interesting dinosaur displays at the Smithsonian, what is found are skulls, bones, teeth, and claws. Usually the fossilized remains consist only of the originally hard parts since the softer parts quickly rot away or are devoured by microorganisms. In addition, the bones are seldom articulated (connected together) and are instead disarticulated (pulled apart). Most dinosaur finds consist of only small portions of any one animal and so paleontologists must play detective to try to determine how the animal was originally put together. For this reason, most museum reconstructed dinosaur skeletons consist of the bones from numerous specimens, as we learned was the case with the *Diplodocus* skeleton at Carnegie. In addition, in many cases the skeletons do not consist of all bones, but have plaster replica casts inserted from other skeletons that may be on display somewhere else. For this reason the museums will often paint the skeletons a color, usually brown, tan, or black, so that it is difficult or impossible to determine which bones are original by just looking at the display.

When paleontologists recover bones at a site they normally make what is called a bone bed map that illustrates which bones were found where. Since dinosaur bone bed maps usually show disarticulation and extreme mixing of the fossilized remains, these maps are excellent evidence for catastrophe. This is evidence that can be interpreted to strongly support the creationist view against the evolutionary view.

The recent depictions of multi-colored dinosaur exteriors envisioned by evolutionists come from their belief that dinosaurs and birds are related. In reality, no way has yet been perfected to determine the color of dinosaur skin. A few fossils have been found that provide additional information about the exteriors of the dinosaurs, such as skin impressions and mummified parts, but these are all quite rare. All of the dinosaur skin impressions that I have seen indicate the exterior parts of the skin of dinosaurs consists of scales.

It is true that a majority of evolutionary paleontologists currently support the hypothesis that birds evolved from dinosaurs. This, of course, cannot be true

Smithsonian Bone Jumbles are an Indicator of Catastrophe

according to the Bible since the birds were created on day five, one day ahead of the animals. A scientific lack of evidence exists for the evolutionary belief that birds have dinosaurs as their ancestors, and this way of thinking has come about in large part due to the recent emphasis on cladistics. The dinosaur skin imprints that have been identified in the last 150 years do not indicate the presence of feathers. The so-called "protofeathers" from China are probably the remains of collagenous fibers that formed feather-looking patterns during decomposition. Relevant remains found of Theropod dinosaurs do not indicate that they had a bird-type lung/diaphragm, but rather that they had a crocodilian-type of breathing apparatus.

God certainly could have designed some dinosaurs to have feathers, but the evidence for that to this point is from the imaginations of those who believe in the concept of dinosaur to bird evolution. If this occurred, scales on the dinosaurs would have had to have evolved into the feathers. It is very doubtful that the DNA for animals with scales would have had the information needed to allow this sort of evolution. I believe this can be categorized as macroevolution, which I have submitted has been proven to be impossible. Compared to the scales of reptiles, bird feathers are very different and extremely more complex.

I do not know of anyone who has disputed the statistics reported by creationists concerning the fossil distribution that strongly points to a marine catastrophe:

- 95% of all fossils are marine invertebrates (no backbones), and are mostly shellfish
- Of the remaining 5%, 95% of those are algae and plant fossils (4.75% of total)
- 95% of the remaining 0.25% consists of other invertebrates, including insects (0.2375%)
- The remaining 0.0125% includes all vertebrates, mostly fish[48]

These statistics are not obvious from a trip through the displays of the Smithsonian, or any other natural history museum, because the relatively rare fossil vertebrate animals are the ones that are seen because they are the most spectacular, especially the dinosaurs! One result is that most people have no idea of the overwhelming quantity and range of the marine invertebrate fossils that have been found in the rock record.

MUSEUM OF THE ROCKIES

The Museum of the Rockies (MOR) is located on the campus of Montana State University in Bozeman, Montana. While it is not among the largest natural history museums, the fossil displays there are among the finest in the world. The dinosaur displays are absolutely wonderful with many Theropods, duckbilled, and other dinosaur specimens beautifully prepared and displayed. There is a fabulous display of dinosaur eggs—the best display that I have ever seen in a museum. I am a fancier of the Ceratopsian dinosaurs, so I was not disappointed to see at

Museum of the Rockies in Bozeman, Montana

the MOR the best display I am aware of showing these horned dinosaurs.

Some evolutionary paleontologists claim close to 1000 different kinds of dinosaurs have been found. I join with creationist experts to conclude that there were no more than about 50 dinosaur kinds. At the MOR I found evidence that supports the smaller number. Among the more familiar Ceratopsians are the *Triceratops, Chasmosaurus, Styracosaurus,* and *Torosaurus* monikers. One of the display signs at the MOR reads, "The skeletons of *Torosaurus* and *Triceratops* are very similar. Except for the skulls, we cannot tell for sure to which animal individual bones belong." That statement confirms my previous studies that the postcranial skeletons of these animals are nearly identical. I think this fact is an indicator that the variability in skulls could simply be as a result of the age and/or gender of each animal. With creationist presuppositions it would be easy to conclude that the horned dinosaurs were just one original kind. There are even similarities in the skulls for the Ceratopsians where they all have about the same teeth, jaw construction, and parrot-like beaks.

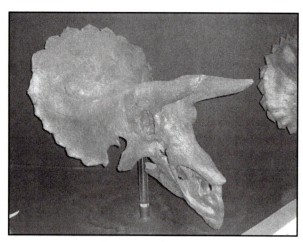

Horned Dinosaur Triceratops Skull

Also displayed at the MOR is the *T-rex* femur from the Wankel specimen in which was found the flexible tissues that skyrocketed the museum and soft tissue discoverer Mary Schweitzer to international acclaim. The most recent sophisticated tests continue to confirm that the tissue was indeed soft, which has caused no lack of consternation among evolutionists. One of the display signs in the MOR about this discovery reads (right next to a photo of Mary's pretty face), "The discovery is also making scientists rethink the way bones fossilize, because with our present understanding of the fossilization process, soft tissue should not exist." According to evolutionary belief the femur bone is 68 million years old and so those holding to methodological naturalism now are left with the task of explaining the unexplainable within their paradigm.

A true scientist with the understanding that science means knowledge would have no problem considering hypotheses that put forth the possibility that the dinosaur is closer to 4,500 years old. Mary says she is a Christian but has not yet considered anything other than a timeline of millions of years for the rock record and what has been found in it. I have no specific facts to confirm this assumption, but I assume that Mary's education track was not much different from the one devised by the authors of *The Evolution Dialogues* for Angela Rawlett.

Broken *T-rex* Femur with Soft tissue

BRIGHAM YOUNG EARTH SCIENCE MUSEUM

This museum has recently been renamed Brigham Young University Museum of Paleontology and is located in Provo, Utah. It is an excellent fossil museum that I would describe as the "museum of giants." I have named it that way because it is primarily a museum of the big, bigger, and biggest specimens of animals and plants found in the rock record. There are giant fish, footprints, stingrays, ammonites, leaves, palm fronds, ground sloths, deer, and mastodons. There are giant dinosaurs of all kinds including Theropods, Sauropods, Ankylosaurs, Stegosaurs, and Ceratopsians. There are giant dinosaur femurs and scapulas that are larger than the human body. Representatives of large extinct mammals such as the *Uintatherium* and *Brontotherium* are also on display.

This display tends to substantiate the observation that lifeforms in the past were often much larger than those today. If there was a yearlong worldwide Flood as the Bible clearly states, we could expect that the environmental and ecological conditions after the Flood would

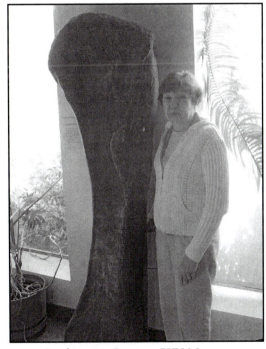

Brachiosaurus Femur at BYU Museum

Large Fossilized Palm Frond at BYU Museum

be much different than those prior to the Flood. It would be logical to assume that all of the plant life we can envision uprooted and floating on the water would have an effect on the carbon dioxide levels.

Some creationists have developed hypotheses that take into account the large size of life with the biblical long ages reported in the Bible and other considerations. It is possible that there would have been a higher proportion of oxygen in the atmosphere prior to the Flood than after. So, a plausible explanation is that the larger life was a result of the higher oxygen levels and that the longer age spans could also be because of the different environment. These are questions that I do not believe can conclusively be answered this side of Heaven.

PREHISTORIC MUSEUM COLLEGE OF EASTERN UTAH

The Prehistoric Museum at the College of Eastern Utah in Price, Utah is another fine museum with many large and important specimens on display. It too holds to the evolution

"Prehistoric" Museum at College of Eastern Utah

and millions of years presuppositions. It is noteworthy that the word *prehistoric* is in the name of the museum. This is noteworthy because for the biblical creationist there is no such thing as prehistoric animals or prehistoric man. Our history starts "in the beginning" as described in Genesis 1:1. Then in chapter one of the book of Genesis the creation of the plants and trees (verses 11-12), birds and sea creatures (verses 20-22), land animals (verses 24-25), and man (verses 26-27) are all described in a historical narrative.

I have often mentioned to Christians that they have allowed the culture to "evolutionize" them. The use of the word *prehistoric* is one example of that fact. When Christians use the words *prehistoric* or *prehistoric man* or *prehistoric animals* they are accepting those atheistic and deistic presuppositions concerning the origin of life and humankind, and at the same time are in effect rejecting the word of God.

A study of the evolution of our English language shows how the atheistic or naturalistic bias has been allowed to change our perception of the Creation. For example, in *A Handy Dictionary of the English Language from Noah Webster*, Ivison, Blakeman, Taylor & Co., New York, 1877, the word *history* is defined as, "a continuous narrative of events." The words *prehistory, prehistoric,* and *natural history* are not even listed in this dictionary. While the definition for the word *history* in more recently published dictionaries has not changed much if at all since 1877, the words not listed in 1877 are now ubiquitous in the current dictionaries. What does this tell us? At the very least it tells us that those words were not at all common in 1877 when the dictionary was published.

Christians have also allowed the secular museums to change the meaning of the descriptive field of study termed *natural history*. These secular museums would have us believe that their depictions of chronological taxonomies and cladistic diagrams prove that they know scientifically the history of their perceived evolution of life over billions of years. This is, of course, as I have been showing in this book, a big lie.

Besides, in my study of recent (published 1995 and 2003) Webster dictionaries, *natural history* is defined as, "the study of the animal, vegetable, and mineral world," or "a treatise on some aspect of nature." There is no insinuation of a chronological component to the definition for the field of *natural history* in these definitions. On the other hand, the definitions for the root word *history* have a definite time component such as found in the definitions that read,

"an account of what has happened, especially in the life of a people, a country etc.," or "the branch of knowledge that deals systematically with the past" or "a known or recorded past." To have history it is a requirement to have a historian or eyewitness to the events being recorded.

Biblical Christians have such an eyewitness to their understanding of history, and that is God Himself who has provided us in the Bible with a history from the beginning of the universe. Those whose faith is based on naturalism (evolution) have no eyewitness to their speculative and ever-changing hypotheses concerning what happened in the past. No wonder, then, that their story varies

Allosaurus Skeleton with Bones Painted Black

in every important aspect from the biblical account. So, I have removed the words *prehistoric, prehistoric animals,* and *prehistoric man* from my spoken vocabulary and correct those Christians that I hear using those words.

At the Price museum, most of the many dinosaur skeletons have all of their bones painted black. The museum does have a very informative display that explains how skeletons are put together for viewing using bones and casts from several sources as I explained earlier regarding the Carnegie Museum. The Price museum is the only museum I have visited that has been so (refreshingly) forthcoming regarding this process. Price is located in Carbon County, Utah, which is named for the vast amounts of coal found and mined in the area. A number of excellent fossils in the museum are made up of coal including tree trunks and dinosaur tracks.

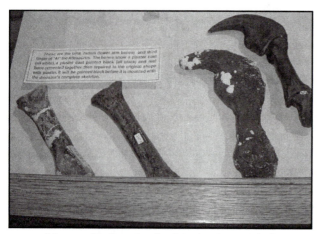

Museum Explanation for Painting Bones Black

In the matter of coal formation, evolutionists and creationists are parsecs apart as far as explanations. Again, it is slow process versus a fast process. Evolutionists believe that coal is formed from peat over long periods of time. Many creationists believe that coal is the result of cataclysmic actions of the worldwide Flood.

With regard to dinosaur tracks, evolutionist authority Martin Lockley writes, "Studies of modern tracks reveal that footprints nevertheless deteriorate rapidly; they are usually destroyed within a few days or weeks."[49] Lockley also writes, "Thus we conclude that the answers to *where* and *how* tracks are preserved are largely geological, not biological. Obviously it is necessary for animals to walk (a biological activity) in order to leave tracks. But the substrate conditions must be suitable in the first place, and then the dynamics of sediment accumulation must be conducive to preservation."[50]

A dinosaur must first walk across sediment that is soft enough to allow the impression of footprints. The footprints must then be quickly covered with additional sediment so as to preserve them. Eventually the prints turn to coal (for the samples at Price), but there remains a boundary layer so that the infill material is easily separated from the footprints. Is this best explained by a slow or a catastrophic process? I am much more comfortable with the catastrophic process.

CREATIONIST MUSEUMS

In many parts of the country there are privately funded natural history museums that, unlike all the taxpayer funded ones, have the courage to provide displays that interpret the universe using the biblical worldview. Biblical Christians should visit and support these museums at every opportunity.

Two of these museums I can wholeheartedly endorse as being worthy of destination visits from anywhere in North America. The first is The Creation Museum, an outreach of Answers in Genesis, which is located near the Cincinnati international airport. For more information you can go to the website www.creationmuseum.org. The other, operated by The Foundation Advancing Creation Truth, is located in Glendive, Montana, with the website www.creationtruth.org.

In those situations where a group or organization would like to bring a creation museum to their location as a part of a creation conference or other event, my website www.creation-engineeringconcepts.org can be accessed to book the "Mitchell Traveling Dinosaur and Fossil Museum." Traveling creation museum visits are also available through Ian Juby at his website www.ianjuby.org.

CHAPTER 9

WHAT IS IN THE FIELD?

IN A SIMILAR manner to chapter eight where I reported on museum findings, this chapter will look at some of the field investigations that I have conducted in the last ten years or so.

FOSSILS OF THE OREGON COAST

My wife and I live near Portland, Oregon, which is just a couple of hours away from the beautiful Oregon Coast. We love to visit the beaches and marvel at the wonders so obvious in the area. I have a collection of seashells that I have picked up mostly from the Oregon beaches and from the many novelty stores at the coast. There are areas at the Oregon Central Coast where it is still legal to collect invertebrate marine fossils. Therefore, I also have a collection of these fossils. From these trips to the coast I have learned two important things that tend to substantiate the biblical worldview.

First, when living clams and other similar shelled types of invertebrates die, their shells open up soon after death. Yet the fossil clams found on the Oregon Coast are generally found with the shells closed. These clams were buried alive! This situation is true not only at the Oregon Coast, but all over the world as well, even on the tops of mountains like Mt. Everest. Here we have another indicator of rapid burial that matches the creationist expectations.

The Magnificent Oregon Coast

Secondly, even though the modern shells and the fossils have been assigned different species names by evolutionary specialists, there are many cases where the modern and the fossil look identical, or nearly identical. Thus, we have a situation of topsy-turvy fossils—fossils that have not changed much, if any, over the supposed 20 million year history that the fossils are assumed to represent.

Fossil Clams Buried Abruptly

These living fossils bring into question the long ages presupposed by evolutionists, and we see in Oregon another example of *stasis* in the fossil record, as pointed out by Stephen Jay Gould (see chapter 3).

The evidence from the Oregon Coast can indeed easily be interpreted to match the predictions and the expectations of the biblical creationist!

JOHN DAY FOSSIL BEDS

In the opposite direction to the Oregon Coast from our home is Central Oregon, an area that includes the John Day Fossil Beds. Located within the confines of the John Day Fossil Beds National Monument is a multi-million dollar fossil museum and visitor center. It is named The Thomas Condon Paleontology Center, but I have nicknamed it "The Church at Sheep Rock." The reason is that the facility is located at the base of a small mountain named Sheep Rock. Because all of the information in the displays and videos, and all the information the rangers disseminate about the evolutionary worldview (religion) of naturalism, the facility is a church for the religion of naturalism. Actually, when it comes to origins I have yet to visit any tax-supported institution that has exhibited anything other than interpretations for that atheistic religion.

What amazed me most, though, was that we were told that science demands assuming uniformitarianism. Some of the information at the center actually states, "The only assumption that we make today is that the principles of nature have been uniform through time. We hasten to stress that this uniformity

Pallisades Formation at John Day Fossil Beds

is an assumption that we make about nature and so is a doctrine rather than a logically proven law."[51] Yet the videos shown and the displays all exhibit nothing but catastrophe! The center's information admits that the John Day area was formed by tremendous volcanic actions with fantastic lava flows over large areas and water events that tended to tear the landscape asunder. As usual, the evidence is stated as proving evolution and millions of years, but in actuality the evidence matches perfectly to the expectations of the creation scientist that there was a worldwide Flood as explained plainly in Genesis.

Between the small town of Fossil, Oregon, and the beautiful geologic formations called the Painted Hills are found a number of small shale hills topped with thick layers of fossil leaf impressions. Experts have identified leaves from maple, alder, beech, pine, elm, grape, redwood, rose, and oak plants. The evolutionary interpretation is that these mounds represent the accumulation of plant debris over a long period of time in situ as volcanic ash precipitated out of lake water. But, the question has to be asked, *where is the rest of the forest that these leaves represent?* No large pieces were found of limbs or trunks. And why would the piles of leaves exist due to some sort of uniformitarian action? We do not see this type of fossil leaf formation

Hill Covered with Leaf Fossils in John Day Monument

currently occurring anywhere in the world. As mentioned, fossilization requires rapid burial and does not happen due to the processes imagined by evolutionists where leaves are slowly covered by precipitation from ash in lake water. The proper interpretation is that the leaves were ripped from the trees and transported by large amounts of water from some other place, then deposited and buried by silt where they are now found. This would, of course, then be consistent with the Genesis Flood model.

Throughout the John Day area are found indications of rapid and large quantities of erosion of the geologic features. This is true of both the volcanic rocks and the sedimentary rocks. This evidence is easier to interpret as the result of catastrophe rather than uniformity. Not far from the Church at Sheep Rock is the beautiful Picture Gorge canyon through which the John Day River courses. The walls of this canyon are steep and in places nearly vertical. The evolutionary interpretation depicted on the taxpayer-funded roadside sign reads, "The sharp, steep walls of Picture Gorge suggest a sudden cataclysm and not the slow, relentless forces that actually shaped it." From this interpretation you would think that someone actually stood by for the supposed millions of years and watched nature form the gorge. But there really was no one there to see the gorge formed and the evolutionary interpretation is double-speak nonsense.

A much more reasonable interpretation would be that the vertical walls of the canyon were indeed cut by a sudden cataclysm and not by a slow process. If the canyon was millions of years old, the steep walls would be rounded or even completely removed by erosion.

Many other evidences in the geology and the paleontology of the John Day Fossil Beds area exist that can easily be interpreted according to creationist presuppositions. For additional and more detailed information, I highly recommend the book *Road Guide to the John Day Area of Central Oregon* referenced at the end of this chapter.

Picture Gorge Canyon

THE GRAND CANYON

My wife and I were privileged to be able to take a rafting trip on the Colorado River through a portion of the Grand Canyon. I am convinced no better trip exists to confirm the creationist interpretations of earth history. Quite a number of creationist books and papers have been written and are readily available concerning the many creationist interpretations of the evidence in and about the Grand Canyon. I am aware of at least 15 strong evidences that point to a catastrophic creation of the Grand Canyon and according to a recent timeline. I would like to focus on some of the evidences that were most impressive to me as I traveled through the canyon.

1. We observed multiple layers of sedimentary rock strata, supposedly representing millions of years, which were folded together. Common sense tells even the geologically ignorant that brittle rock cannot be folded without cracking. This indicates that the layers must have been folded while they were still damp or wet and not yet solidified. This also means that the folded deposits had to be part of a single event and not multiple events spread out over millions of years.

Folded Sedimentary Layers at the Grand Canyon

2. According to uniformitarian geology a buried erosion surface that separates two layers of supposed different ages represents millions of years of "missing" time. These surfaces are called unconformities. In the Grand Canyon I was shown the *Great Unconformity* at the bottom of the canyon sedimentary layers, and it looked nearly perfectly flat with no indication of erosional gouges or grooves that I could see. The basement rocks of granite and schist looked to have been planed off to this flat condition. One can only imagine the energy required to do this; I suggest that the cataclysmic forces of a yearlong worldwide Genesis Flood would have been capable.

The Great Unconformity at the Grand Canyon

3. The Grand Canyon exhibited vertical-walled side canyons similar to the one I described in the John Day area (Picture Gorge) and that have no evidences of water sources sufficient to have formed them. One would expect to find much rock debris in the bottoms of these canyons if their formation took millions of years, but very little exists. These evidences speak strongly against the millions-of-years paradigm and are consistent with a catastrophic formation.

4. Throughout the West in the United States have been found numerous Indian petroglyphs and pictographs. Petroglyphs are patterns that have been chipped or carved into rock, and pictographs are patterns that have been painted on the rock. Some of these images look just like dinosaurs. Indian experts have no problem identifying the animals depicted in most of these pictures, but whenever the animal looks like a dinosaur, its description officially becomes a total mystery. This is understandable if your presuppositions preclude the possibility that men ever saw dinosaurs.

Indian Pictographs in the Grand Canyon

One explanation is that vandals drew the pictures and they are frauds, but if that is the case, the value of all Indian pictographs and petroglyphs would be reduced to nothing. There would be no reason to spend effort to protect these examples of ancient art. On our Grand Canyon rafting trip, we were being shown a number of these pictographs thought to have been left on the canyon walls by the Anasazi Indians, when one of the children in our group exclaimed, "Look up there … it's a dinosaur." On the sheer face of the canyon wall about 15 feet above our heads was a pictograph that looked just like a Sauropod dinosaur! I have not heard any claims that these particular art remnants are fraudulent, so if authentic this Sauropod is evidence that the Anasazi Indians from 500 to 1500 years ago had seen dinosaurs.

HELL CREEK FORMATION

Several years ago my wife and I were able to participate in a dinosaur dig in the Hell Creek Formation near Glendive, Montana. In that dig we came away with a prized possession of the Mitchell Traveling Dinosaur and Fossil Museum, a large portion of a *Triceratops* rib. Also in Glendive is The Glendive Dinosaur and Fossil Museum, which is the second largest dinosaur museum in Montana. It is different from the MOR in that all displays are interpreted according to biblical presuppositions.

Digging Dinosaur Bones in the Hell Creek Formation

The official (governmental evolutionary) explanation for the Hell Creek Formation is, "About 65 million years ago, the inland sea receded as the Rocky Mountains rose, pushing the shoreline further east. Great rivers meandered through the coastal plain in a warm and humid climate, depositing sediment which would later become known as the Hell Creek Formation. The tan sandstones, siltstones, and mudstones are common throughout eastern Montana, but can be best seen in road cuts along the highway… Dinosaur fossils are frequently found in the Hell Creek Formation…"[52]

The obvious problems with this interpretation are:

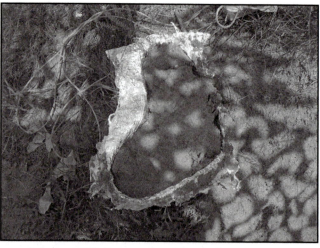

Triceratops Rib Recovered and Ready for Preparation

- The Hell Creek Formation is subject to continuous and large amounts of erosion. If the sediments representing this formation were laid down 65 million years ago, there wouldn't be anything left of them at the current rate of erosion. The reason we find so many dinosaur parts in the formation sediments is because the erosion is constantly uncovering new bones, claws, skulls, and teeth.
- Meandering rivers are not known to create fossils. The technical literature is very consistent in stating that fossilization normally requires rapid deposition. How did all of the dinosaur bones end up in the formation sediments from meandering rivers, no matter how great they were? So far as I know, no fossils have been found in the remnants of the great Missoula Flood that formed the scablands of eastern Washington. There was tremendous geologic activity caused by much water and ice movement over a short period of time in the Missoula Flood, yet with scant (if any) fossil evidence left behind.

Whenever and wherever I look in the rock record, I see evidence of large amounts of water moving quickly over vast land areas. Those who are committed to the faith of methodological naturalism must go to great extents to imagine scenarios where tranquil floods, rivers, and lakes have caused all of the buried fossil geological evidence. The Genesis Flood is a much more satisfying explanation!

YELLOWSTONE NATIONAL PARK

I have visited Yellowstone National Park three times in my life. The natural geological and biological sights there are wonderful to behold and provide ample opportunity to consider the many things in God's General Revelation that have been provided for our enjoyment and education. Literally thousands of books have already been published on this place and there is not room in this book to expand a lot on my Yellowstone findings and opinions. However, I do have one park observation that is pertinent to the topic of origins that I would like to mention.

The last time my wife and I visited Yellowstone, we were amazed at the numbers of Bison in evidence. It seemed they were everywhere we went and were quite a nuisance to the traffic

Scenic Wonders of Yellowstone National Park

flow through the park. I have read that there were over 100 million of these beasts roaming the Great Plains until they were slaughtered by the "taming of the west." As a result they were almost driven to extinction by man. None of those 100 million or so bison that were killed a century ago have left any remains in the rock record; fossilized or otherwise. Observation shows us animals that die are ripped apart by scavengers and soon every atom of their bodies is dispersed. Uniformitarianism attempts to tell us that the present explains the past, but the present cannot explain, among many other things, the "billions of dead things buried in rock layers laid down by water all over the earth." Bison skeletons are not piling up around us by the thousands, and this is true of every other form of life in existence today.

Bison on the Road in Yellowstone

CLEVELAND-LLOYD DINOSAUR QUARRY

The Cleveland-Lloyd Dinosaur Quarry is a National Natural Landmark administered by the Bureau of Land Management and located about 30 miles south of Price, Utah. Access to the fairly remote site is via 12 miles of mostly graveled county road. Reopened in 2007 after 20 months of renovations, the visitor center is the first one that the BLM ever had. "More than 12,000 individual bones and one dinosaur egg have come from this prolific fossil bed. It is likely that many 'complete skeletons' have been recovered, although it is impossible to state that with certainty because the bones are in a disarticulated state."[53]

Bone Bed Map at Cleveland-Lloyd Dinosaur Quarry

At our visit in 2009, inside the new visitor's center was a brand new reconstruction of the relatively common *Allosaurus* dinosaur skeleton. The dinosaur (with all black bones) was displayed in the position of chasing after a prey with (according to the current supposition) its tail nearly horizontal to the ground. For decades the Theropod dinosaurs were shown with their massive tails dragging on the ground but new information and interpretations have made that depiction out of date.

Another very interesting aspect of the display was that the animal had a furcula anchored to the upper portion of its ribcage. Experts have recently come to believe that all Theropods had furculas, which were previously placed on the wrong parts of the skeletons in the many reconstructions of these animals. This was monumentally important to my research on the *Archaeopteryx* and added evidentiary weight to my findings that *Archaeopteryx* could not fly and probably was not a bird … just because it may have had a furcula. For more information, including the other reasons for my conclusions about this lifeform, see "*Archaeopteryx*: What Was it?" DVD.[54]

Allosaurus Skeleton at Cleveland-Lloyd Dinosaur Quarry

When we walked into the Cleveland-Lloyd visitor center we were greeted by two young rangers. Since there was only one other couple at the center at the time, and they had already headed out toward the quarry site, my wife and I were courteously latched onto by a male ranger so he could explain the displays. We were glad to have his interest in our education and so we quickly followed him to a large poster displayed on the wall, which was a bone map of all the thousands of disarticulated bones that had been retrieved from the quarry over the years. The ranger told us that scientists had absolutely no idea how all of the bones had ended up in such a tremendous bone jumble—it was a "total mystery." I said, "It is no mystery to me." The ranger looked at me with a startled look on his face, and asked me to explain. I told him that I was a creation scientist and that I believed that the evidence at Cleveland-Lloyd was consistent with the

One of the Dig Sites at Cleveland-Lloyd Dinosaur Quarry

global Flood of Noah's day. He looked stunned and then slowly turned on his heel and walked away. We never saw him again.

We continued to move around the displays near the entrance as I took photographs and my wife took notes. A couple minutes after the interchange with the male ranger, the woman ranger (who was still standing at the entrance counter), said to me, "Did I hear you say that you think the quarry bones are the result of Noah's Flood?" I walked over to her and began providing some additional information on the biblical creationist worldview, but she quickly interrupted me and said, "But that's not scientific!" She quietly listened as I explained the difference between

the definition of science as "knowledge" and the definition of science as "naturalism." After about 5 minutes of explanation she looked at me and said, "Please stop! I don't want to hear any more."

At that point our conversation was over and I walked away to join my wife and to enjoy the rest of the exhibits. The foregoing account is typical of where people have been indoctrinated rather than educated. Unfortunately, that is what happened to me in my formal education and it took years to throw off the evolutionary blindfold so I could see the light. It is also what the AAAS and other

Dinosaur Bone in situ near Cleveland-Lloyd Quarry

evolutionist organizations are attempting to foist upon all public school children. Whether or not my encounter with these two young people will have any positive results I will probably never know. I can pray that I may have planted a seed that would allow one or both of them to use

their minds as they continue their educations and evaluate the many belief systems that abound in the world.

ARCHES NATIONAL PARK

The beauty of the geological formations at Arches National Park near Moab, Utah is among the most fabulous in the world. The 2,000 natural arches in the park, we are told, formed through millions of years of slow erosion carving each arch. The rock units in the park are the ones in which dinosaur bones

Some of the Many Arches at Arches National Park

are often found and, according to the official evolutionary interpretation, represent 300 million years of geologic activity.

I tell anyone who will listen that when they look at these geological formations "they should think catastrophic flood!" Here are the official evolutionary descriptions for the origins of the different rock units in Arches National Park starting with the lowest unit and working up to the highest unit:

- Restricted inland sea
- Offshore marine
- Stream-deposited alluvial fans
- Streams on a vast floodplain
- Wind-deposited dunes
- Streams
- Wind-deposited dunes

- Marginal marine tidal flats
- Coastal marine mudflats
- Streams and floodplains
- Lakes and streams
- Streams
- Rivers on a broad coastal plain
- Stagnant sea[55]

These "rock units" are hundreds of feet thick and are presupposed to consist of identifiable homogeneous layers that took millions of years for each one to form. According to uniformity "the present is the key to the past," but I do not see anything like this going on today. Notice also that most of these units are hypothesized to have their origin with the assistance of water. Even the wind-deposited dunes would have required the addition of water to have solidified into rock.

The official position is that the many arches are assumed to have taken millions of years to form. In our visit to the park, new arches were pointed out by the park signs as just starting to be formed and in various stages of formation. However, the arches are disintegrating at a rate that has resulted in humans being able to witness the destruction of many of them since the start of the 20th century. As many as 40 of the arches have collapsed since 1970! If the arches are supposed to take millions of years to form, but collapse at a rate of, say, 100 per century why would there be any left for us to see? Again, when you look at Arches National Park, consider the evidence and think catastrophic flood, not millions of years.

Not far from Arches National Park is the Copper Ridge area where distinct Sauropod and Theropod dinosaur footprints are found. At

An Arches National Park Interpretive Sign Explaining Collapse

our visit to the site we noticed that the Sauropod trackway is unique in that there is an abrupt change in direction of the tracks. Most dinosaur trackways are quite straight as if the animals

were on a mission to get from one place to another in a hurry. Since there are a few Theropod tracks not far away, one could conclude that the change of direction of the Sauropod tracks was due to the presence of the other animal.

One uniformitarian interpretation of the formation of these trackways is that, "It generally takes millions of years for sediments to turn to rock."[56] Do I know for sure exactly how or when these dinosaur trackways were formed? No, I do not, but the evolutionary presumption aforementioned I am sure is very much in error. I have personally seen wet mud

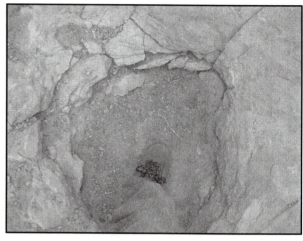

Sauropod Dinosaur Footprint near Moab, Utah

sediments turn into hard rock in less than one year. When one believes the millions of years paradigm, many errors are bound to result. It is consistent with the evidence that the footprints at Copper Ridge could be less than 5,000 years old which would perfectly match the biblical

creationist expectation. At the current rate of deterioration, these particular trackways could be unidentifiable within one more generation due to weather-caused erosion and the many footsteps by visitors to the unprotected site.

DINOSAUR NATIONAL MONUMENT

The first time I visited Dinosaur National Monument near Vernal, Utah, was during the summer prior to my entering high school in 1959. I had looked forward to the visit for months as I had memorized every dinosaur name in Edwin H. Colbert's classic *Dinosaur Book* (published 1951) as well as all of the

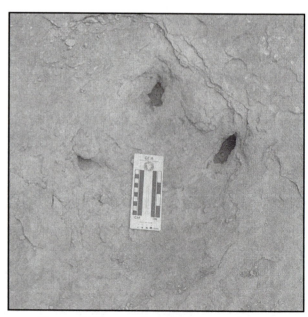

Theropod Dinosaur Footprint near Moab, Utah

creature names in Roy Chapman Andrews' book *All about Dinosaurs*. I felt I had accomplished the coup of the century by convincing my parents to take a detour to the site on the way home from one of our automobile trips to visit relatives in southwest Colorado.

The modern glass-enclosed visitor center at the monument was the coolest place I had ever been in with paleontologists in white coveralls climbing all over a huge rock wall absolutely filled with dinosaur bones. (Eventually 1,600 dinosaur bones were uncovered at the wall for visitors to gaze at from a safe distance behind a sturdy handrail.[57]) I was able to explain to my family, with great authority I might add, all about how the various bones had been buried at that location due to some mysterious geologic action over 100 million years ago. There was no way that I could have believed anything about the past except for evolution and millions of years because everything I had read in books and everything I had seen at all the natural history museums interpreted previous history according to that paradigm. At the young age of fifteen I was thoroughly indoctrinated.

Quarry Site is Closed Due to Safety Hazards

Fifty years later I made my second visit to the monument. Some things had not changed but some things had changed a lot in that half century interval. The things that had not changed were that all government/academia sponsored national parks, national monuments, and museums continue to be driven by the naturalistic faith. Hutton, Lyell, Darwin, and Huxley are still the icons of history for these shrines of evolution. That is still the case at Dinosaur National Monument.

The things that have changed are that the Quarry Visitor Center has been closed since 2006 due to serious life and safety hazards caused by the movement of its foundations, and so visitors can no longer view the large wall of bones. We were able to take a bus from a temporary visitor area

The Geologic Formation in which the Fossils are Found at DNM

and then a walk to an adjacent area where bones still in the sandstone matrix made up of many small pebbles can be seen "up close and personal." For those willing to take the time and make the effort, the walk was probably a better educational experience than if they had been confined to a viewing platform some 20 feet away from the bones in the quarry center.

My worldview had changed to a position diametrically opposite to the one I had 50 years prior. With a different worldview and its associated presuppositions, my interpretations were also different as well. Here is what I saw at Dinosaur National Monument on my last visit:

- Throughout the sandstone rocks of the quarry are found thousands and thousands of fresh water clams. In fact these clams are much more prevalent than the dinosaur bones. These clams look about the same as clams that exist today in fresh waters.

- The various fossils in the quarry are a real jumble. Various kinds of life are in a state of mixed up and mixed in disarticulation. Found besides the dinosaur bones are clams, snails, logs, and wood fragments, which indicate water transportation from somewhere else to where they have been found.

Clam Fossils Mixed in with Dinosaur Bones

- The bones and other fossils are confined to just a certain rock type in the more general Morrison Formation. In other words, the fossils are not spread out over a large area, and one can search areas around the quarry and find few or no fossils. The quarry where the fossils are found is restricted to an area about 50 feet thick by about half a mile long. The entire Morrison Formation encompasses an area of about 700 thousand square miles, including most of Montana, Wyoming, and Colorado, as well as substantial portions of adjoining states.

- There has not been found in the quarry matrix any of the types of food

Large *in situ* Dinosaur Bone at DNM

that one would speculate large dinosaurs require to survive. This is another indicator that the fossils are not in situ as standard evolutionary explanations require.

From these observations and others by qualified creation scientists,[58] it is clear that the quarry deposit is an example of a tremendous watery catastrophe. Evidence, I believe, consistent with the Genesis Flood!

FOSSIL BUTTE NATIONAL MONUMENT

Fossil Butte National Monument (FBNM) is located amidst the huge Green River Formation not far from the little town of Kemmerer, Wyoming. The Green River Formation covers large areas of Utah, Wyoming, and Colorado. Evolutionists have speculated that at the time of the fossilization of the Green River life forms, a number of large lakes existed covering much of the area that somehow created conditions that resulted in millions of fossils, mostly fish.[59] Creationists would presuppose that the many fossils are more likely the result of the Genesis Flood some 4,500 years ago. Near FBNM is an area identified as the Fossil Lake area where there are two types of quarries where fossils are found. The F1 type of quarries exhibit varves or thin sedimentary layers; and the F2 Split Fish type of quarries are without varves.

As noted, fossilization is a rare and exceptional event and requires rapid burial. There is, in fact, no indication that fossilization normally occurs at all in this day and age. Dead marine life is never seen to be turning into fossils at the bottoms of lakes, rivers, or seas. The fossils found in the Southwest Wyoming area can bring hundreds or thousands of dollars depending on the type and quality of the fossils. Evolutionist fossil hunters also take advantage of the supposed age of the fossils (40 million years) in order to attempt to increase their value to prospective buyers. I know that many fossil and mineral sellers stick to the millions of years paradigm solely because of the common perception that something millions of years old is worth a lot more than something only thousands of years old.

It is a fact that most of the fish found fossilized in the limestone matrix in this area are herring or perch types. These fossil fish have different species names from the modern herring and perch fish, but look a lot like them.

Fossil Fish Quarry near Kemmerer, Wyoming

Interestingly enough there are sufficient quantities of these fish still available so that most of the fossils found at Fossil Lake Quarry are discovered, retrieved, and prepared by independent professional fossil hunters. These people make a living by finding, preparing, and selling these fossils to collectors and museums all over the world. As amateurs, my wife and I were able to contract with a group of these professionals and dig for fossils ourselves.

Limestone Slab with Fish Fossils

An amazing find in the quarry was the large number of exploded fish that are encased in the limestone layers. The first fossil that my wife found in our fossil dig at an F2 split fish quarry was an exploded fish. Most hunters would discard these fish as worthless due to their philosophical paradigm or their ignorance of the significance shown by the fossils. As a result of our dig, I kept three of these exploded fish to show in my presentations and in the traveling museum as examples of rapid complete burial of the fish. These exploded fish reinforce the creationist view and destroy uniformitarianism in the rock record at the Wyoming quarries. Experiments and observations of dead fish of today have resulted in the conclusion that they decay within days (or weeks at most) after death.[60] These exploded fish fossils seem to be a snap-shot of time ... the time when they were instantly buried in a catastrophic event!

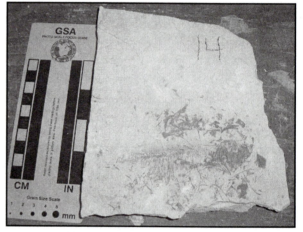

Exploded Fish Fossil in Limestone Rock

We also found lots of fish coprolites in the limestone. Coprolites are another find that most of the fossil hunters discard or dig out as being worthless. But, fish coprolites are an even better evidence of rapid burial than the exploded fish. This is because fish faeces have been determined by experiment to decompose in about one day.[61] Therefore, the fish faeces must have been preserved in the limestone within 24 hours of the time it was deposited in the water by the fish. At FBNM museum were displayed, in addition to many fish, some other (less common) fossils that have been found in the Green River Formation. Examples are turtles, snakes, cattails, berries, leaves,

Coprolite in Fish Fossil Limestone

flowers, March flies, dragonflies, bats, seeds, and a few birds. Most of the non-fish fossils at the museum were cast replicas of the fossils and not the actual fossils themselves due to the value and scarcity of the non-fish fossils.

While I am not able to put forth a comprehensive explanation for the Green River Formation in general or the Fossil Lake area fossils in particular, I believe that the evidence for catastrophe is so well documented to make the evolutionary explanations of slow processes over long periods of time worthless. Time after time when I have looked at the paleontological and geological evidences in my travels to museums and parks I see nothing but catastrophe and residual evidences of massive hydraulic, tectonic, and volcanic actions. Coupling those findings with the overwhelming lack of any evidence for transitional fossil forms in the rock record leads me to conclude that the biblical creationist presuppositions are consistently supportable. This world is explained by creation, not by evolution. Christians can indeed be confident in the Bible from the very first verse! There is nothing in God's Word about the secular conjectures concerning multiple past and future extinctions. What Christians can know, upon our Creator's return, is that they will be joyfully included in the new creation with a new heaven and a new earth. "He will wipe every tear from their eyes. There will be no more death or mourning or crying or pain, for the old order of things [will be] passed away" (Revelation 21:4).

BIG BONE LICK STATE PARK

In Northwest Kentucky, not far from The Answers in Genesis Creation Museum, is what is called "the cradle of American Paleontology." Now designated as a state park, this ancient animal salt lick has been offering up fossil bones to American paleontologists since the time of Ben Franklin and Thomas Jefferson. Many of the animal species found there are similar to those found in La Brea such as American mastodon, Columbian mammoth, and Harlan's ground sloth. However, also found have been numerous extant species including many domesticated such as cows, dogs, horses, sheep, and pigs.

A long history of discovery has resulted in many people being able to put forth their opinions about the origination of the lick and the animals found in it. In 1831 William Cooper reported in his "Notices of Bone Lick" that "the great majority of Big Bone Lick fossils showed some mark of having been subjected to violent action … it is rare to meet with a single bone of the large animals, or of those smaller ones, that accompany them that is not more or less bruised or broken." Cooper concluded that the bones exhibited evidence of the occurrence of a catastrophe that had been a deluge of biblical proportions that drowned the species and relocated their remains at the Lick.[62]

In May of 1842 Charles Lyell visited Big Bone Lick,[63] and from that date evolution and uniformitarianism became the basis of the "official" reports about the site. The disarticulated and scattered condition of the bones makes it difficult for secular scientists to provide a reasonable interpretation for the findings. Nevertheless, as with other public fossil locations throughout the United States, the usual atheistic presuppositions provide the basis for all official interpretations in the Big Bone Lick literature and museum signs.

I have not been able to find any resources that indicate creation scientists have studied the Big Bone Lick evidence or provided scientific interpretations of the site. If and when that occurs I expect the findings could be similar to those that resulted from the work of Mr. Weston at the La Brea Tar Pits.

FURTHER READING

1. Bokovoy, Dennis et al, *Road Guide to the John Day Area of Central Oregon*, Creation Research Society, 2004.
2. Coffin, Harold et al, *Road Guide to Yellowstone National Park and Adjacent Areas*, Creation Research Society, 2005.
3. Reed, John K. & Oard, Michael J., *The Geologic Column—Perspectives within Diluvial Geology*, Creation Research Society Books, 2006.
4. Vail, Tom et al, *Your Guide to the Grand Canyon—A Different Perspective*, Master Books, 2008.
5. Whitcomb, John C., *The World that Perished*, Baker Book House, 1988.

CHAPTER 10

CONTEMPORARY STANCES TOWARD EVOLUTION

ANGELA'S STORY

WE HAVE PREVIOUSLY examined the evolutionists' argument that since many liberal Christians are able to accept evolution into their faith, then Biblical Christians should do the same. In chapter 8 of *The Evolution Dialogues* the authors introduce the similar argument that because some Jews and some Muslims are able to accept evolutionary concepts, evolution should be palatable for Biblical Christians. It is presented as a matter of diversity now, but the argument is no more valid than it ever was. The fundamental issue is one of Truth and not one of compatibility or compromise. Either Jesus is the only way to the Father or He isn't. If one believes that He is, then it would be consistent to follow the many directives He has provided us in His Word. It would be consistent to believe that His words would be truthful and correct.

Angela is now open to the evolution of life elsewhere in the universe due to many months of evolutionary indoctrination by her instructors and advisors concerning the presupposed evolution of life on earth. The question now is: Are there any doctrines or even basic teachings of the Bible that she would still unquestionably accept? My expectation from my experience is that the answer would be no.

I took a Christian-based "Critical Thinking" university level course once where the students were instructed to critically examine a number of controversial issues. What was amazing to me was that some of the issues that we examined in the course (such as evolution vs. creation) were presented in a manner that taught these issues could be understood from some sort of a neutral position. The instruction at least implied that a true critical thinker would strive to find that neutral position so that he would be able to better understand the issues involved and then come to a truthful and unbiased conclusion about it. What I could see was that there is

111

no such thing as a neutral, unbiased position, especially with regard to evolution vs. creation. The neutral position most asked of biblical creationists (even in many Christian courses) is for them to step away from God's Word and look at the origins evidence solely from the naturalistic viewpoint. It should be obvious that when one does that, they no longer have any godly presuppositions left to their worldview and the argument is lost before it starts. So just like the word "science" the word "neutral" has some very different definitions depending on your bias. This critical-thinking "definition game" can be confusing, and the Christian must be aware of it at all times so as to not be misled.

Speaking of definitions, the word *altruism* is normally defined as, "unselfish regard or concern for or devotion to the welfare of others." An evolutionist definition is, "an instinctive cooperative behavior that is detrimental to the individual but increases the fitness of other members of the species."[64] There are some concepts hidden in these two differing definitions that I would like to look at more carefully.

So far as human behavior is concerned, much evidence exists that altruism is a learned behavior. I know of no infant that knows about sharing without the instruction of those who are older. Similarly, God has provided the Golden Rule and other instruction in His Word so that all mankind can be taught that they are to love others as they love themselves. These examples discredit the evolutionist belief that altruism in humans is instinctive and that altruism exists as a result of an evolutionary process. In a way, the evolutionary definition for altruism is another circular argument. This is because evolution is a philosophy that proposes that change comes about through random processes of mutation and selection (survival of the fittest) and so there should be no action taken by any organism that could be interpreted as contrary to its own survival. But then, the many cooperative relationships and actions that are observed in nature are explained as a result of evolution. What could be more obvious is that these cooperative behaviors are designed by God to meet His plan for the synergistic operation of the universe. Mankind is treated in a different manner by God than is the rest of life since he is not an animal and has been designed (in the image of God) with the capability to communicate with the Creator. In addition, evolutionists have no answer for how animal instincts could ever have evolved. The story that it just came about through some mysterious random process of DNA gaining information over long periods of time is unsupported by true science as well as God's Word. Mutations and natural selection cannot have done this, but God could have and did.

If Angela were really capable of critical thinking she would be able to see the worthlessness of the evolutionary philosophy in the quote provided her by the hypothetical Muslim professor who said, "Evolution science raises new questions with every new finding." How true that statement is. Every past evolutionary link has been disproved and every present and future link will be disproved. It won't be long until the evolutionary development of men from apes will not require any links (since there aren't any), so evolution will drop the requirement for their existence. Every evolutionary hypothesis has fundamental weaknesses that are easy to see and that even evolutionists agree exist. There is no hypothesis, however, that could ever disprove the theory of evolution in the minds of its adherents since no matter what the evidence is, the philosophy is stretched to fit the belief; it must be true since the presuppositions in operation in methodological naturalism require that it be true.

So Angela will be presented with one interpretation stated as a fact (ISF) after another until there is nothing regarding reality that is absolute. All of the evidence will answer no questions for her because she will be driven further from her Bible, and the question marks next to God in her brain will finally cancel Him out. She will become another fool without excuse.

"For since the creation of the world God's invisible qualities—his eternal power and divine nature—have been clearly seen, being understood from what has been made, so that men are without excuse. For although they knew God, they neither glorified him as God nor gave thanks to him, but their thinking became futile and their foolish hearts were darkened. Although they claimed to be wise, they became fools" (Romans 1:20-22).

Contemporary Stances toward Evolution

A Touchy Subject

Scientific Creationism

Intelligent Design

In the discussion of controversial matters, most thinking people like to believe they are open-minded to the facts and logical in their conclusions. As mentioned earlier, university courses in critical thinking skills exist to help students understand fair-mindedness, intellectual humility, and intellectual integrity as they ponder tough life subjects and concepts.

All thinkers should indeed develop, and then improve, their critical thinking skills. It is also my observation that in the evolution versus creation argument, there can be some on both sides who lack this particular skill. But, as I follow the vehement anti-creationist arguments in the scientific literature and in the general secular media, I am astounded at the lack of critical thinking displayed therein. There are at least six popular distortion techniques commonly used by evolutionists that Christians must be keenly aware of to be able to defend the faith (1Peter 3:15) and understand the truth regarding scientific evidence in the origins debate. The six distortion techniques are:

Distortion Technique #1. The BLIND APPEAL TO AUTHORITY

This technique is usually the first used to discredit creation science and creation scientists. In this technique, the creation science position is dismissed with a wave of the hand by statements such as "no real scientist believes..." or "all experts are in accord that..." A very common example of this technique is where an evolutionary proponent will say that evolution is a proven scientific fact and anyone who does not believe this is ignorant or an idiot.

A look at history reveals that most major breakthroughs in science occurred because some researcher probed outside the prevailing opinion. A critical thinker will always agree with the statement that "truth is not determined by majority opinion."

Distortion Technique #2. *AD HOMINEM* ATTACKS

This technique is often used by anti-creationists against creation scientists and other creation science proponents. *Ad hominem* is Latin and means "to the man." In other words, the attack used in this technique is in the form of personal attacks or insults that have nothing to do with the evidence. It is not surprising that this technique is so popular among anti-creationists since the evidence for macroevolution is so weak. And the weaker the evidence is, the louder the personal attacks and insults usually are by those who use *ad hominem* attacks. I have personally been accused of being "unethical" because my creationist beliefs are at odds with the evolutionary worldview.

Evolutionists say, for another example, that a certain creation scientist believes in God or the Bible; therefore, he is biased and anything he says on the subject of origins cannot be trusted or is not scientific. It would be just as incorrect for a creationist to say evolutionists do not believe in God, therefore they are biased and anything they say on the subject of origins cannot be trusted. Everyone is biased and evolution scientists (most of whom rely on funding that requires agreement with naturalistic interpretations) are among the most highly biased of all.

Both sides in the debate must rely on the quality and testability of the scientific evidence to determine the validity of an interpretation, hypothesis, or theory. With origins science, the presuppositions that are foundational to a hypothesis or theory must be known and understood before the interpretation can be evaluated by anyone for possible truth.

Distortion Technique #3. SELECTIVE USE OF EVIDENCE

People will believe anything. This is because there are always ways to find or concoct evidence to support any position, no matter how ridiculous. If one uses critical thinking skills in an attempt to find truth, then *all* of the relevant evidence must be examined.

For example, the largest gap between evolutionists and creationists in the study of the fossil record is as a result of the refusal by evolutionists to consider the possibility that the fossil record was caused by a worldwide flood. On the other hand, creationists must continually examine the evolutionary view since the vast majority of geology, biology, and paleontology is reported using that view. But evolutionists *never* consider the biblical view. They are examining the evidence while refusing to consider all presuppositions and possibilities. This is one result of their blind faith acceptance of the presuppositions required for methodological naturalism.

Distortion Technique #4. The STRAW MAN

The entire creation vs. evolution debate concerns determination of the truth about the past. When someone distorts a position, and then attacks the distorted position, it is called "attacking a straw man." Anti-creationists constantly set up a straw man attack by trying to make the controversy an issue of religion vs. science. Of course by now we all know that at the outset they define creationism as religion and evolutionism (naturalism) as science.

Another place where anti-creationists set up a straw man attack is concerning creation science and intelligent design biology in the public schools. The humanist detractors will state that creationists are trying to set up religion in the schools when the reality is that creationists simply want the truth about the shortcomings of naturalism taught in addition to the philosophy of naturalism. It is an unfortunate fact that in most public schools and many Christian schools, naturalism is taught as a fact rather than as a philosophy or religion. The AAAS is a vocal and consistent advocate for this kind of indoctrination in our schools.

The current state of public schools in the United States is that the religion of Christianity has indeed been taken out and has been replaced with the religion of Secular Humanism, which has naturalism as its foundation. This outcome was in large part the result of anti-Christians successfully using the straw man attack against the improper interpretation of the concept of separation of church and state.

Distortion Technique #5. BEGGING THE QUESTION

When someone "begs the question" it means that they ask a question to which they have already assumed an answer. Anti-creationists presuppose that there is no God (atheism) or that God is irrelevant (deism), that evolution is true, that homology proves evolution, that creation is a myth, and that there has never been a worldwide flood. In other words, they presuppose that there is no God or that God never supernaturally intervenes into nature.

By defining science to exclude God, evolutionists have begged the question by eliminating one possibility before even starting the debate; therefore, there can be no possibility for honest debate on the issue or for any search for real truth. There is no possibility for dialogue!

Distortion Technique #6. The TESTABLE CONCLUSION

When someone makes a statement that cannot be scientifically tested, it is at most an interpretation or a statement of faith, not of fact. All of our secular museums, our national monuments, and our national parks provide us with interpretations of the earth's past based on the naturalistic worldview. All interpretations are based on presuppositions that may or may not be true. It is important to determine the presuppositions for all of these interpretations presented as facts (ISF).

Famous atheist astronomer Carl Sagan said, "The Cosmos is all there is, or ever was, or ever will be." He stated this as a fact, but this was really just his opinion, which he had taken on faith. This statement is not science since it cannot be scientifically tested. All people, and Christians especially, must ever be vigilant of statements presented as facts that are only interpretations or opinions. This vigilance is a mark of a person who uses developed critical thinking skills.

In chapter eight of *The Evolution Dialogues* the lack of critical thinking is obvious. The authors write regarding the many arguments of creation science that indicate the weaknesses of evolutionary theory, "All of these claims were quickly rebutted by scientists either as erroneous on their face or as distortions of genuine science" (p. 157). One page later they write, "Proponents of 'intelligent design' claim that ID is science, although there is no actual research to support this claim." In statements like these can be seen aspects of multiple distortion techniques.

Probably the most revealing quote in the entire book, however, is where the authors write on page 161, "(For evolutionary biologists, micro- and macroevolution are equivalent, differing only with regard to timescale and accompanying degree of biological modification.)" This is the point that I have been pounding throughout this book! Christians cannot lose sight of this fact and must understand it means that those who accept evolution into their faith will indeed be accepting this presupposition and all of its accompanying atheistic baggage as well. For Christians to do that is nothing but a tragic mistake!

It must not be forgotten either that many of the scientists who are in the forefront of the attempt to convince Christians that they can accept evolution and millions of years into their faith are avowed atheists. One of these is Eugenie Scott who is director of the National Center for Science Education and one of members of the editorial advisory board for *The Evolution Dialogues*. She is a perfect example of a person who uses the disingenuous rhetoric calling for "dialogue" when she really means "no dialogue." In 1996, she advised evolutionists to never debate creationists because they would "probably get beaten."[65] For a long period prior to the time of her coming out with this opinion, creationists like Henry Morris and Duane Gish had conducted scores of winning debates with evolutionists. Since then the number of these debates has been reduced to a fraction of the previous amount. The reason for this reduction is not the unwillingness of creationists. Does this sound like the evolutionist faction is open to dialogue?

The late Stephen Jay Gould was a Marxist and another person that a Christian would do well to ignore regarding opinions on the relationship of science to religion. In his Marxist worldview, it would make sense that life could pop into being. He did not see the gradualism in the fossil record that is a foundation for evolution. Thus he developed his theory of punctuated equilibrium. How interesting it is that evolutionists will accept dialogue about Gould's ideas, which are counter to the whole concept of gradual evolution over millions of years, but will not discuss intelligent design or a Designer. At the very least this is inconsistent thinking, but I would say it is also not critical thinking.

Ken Miller is another member of the editorial advisory board for *The Evolution Dialogues*. He displays a great ability to make up stories when he attempts to explain the evolution of the complex eye from a few light-sensitive cells (p.165). This, however, is not science; it is science fiction. Each one of the steps he so imaginatively describes would in reality require thousands of carefully directed changes. Understand that, unless an eye is fully developed, it would not provide sight and so there would be no reason for natural selection to operate to select for it. Any change that did not provide sight would be totally useless. The mutations imagined by Miller would have all been eliminated by natural selection and the complex eye would not result. No, a much more reasonable explanation is that there is a Creator who designed and created each type of eye.

For the authors to use a keystone arch (p. 166) as an example to prove the method for the natural development of irreducible complexity in lifeforms is ludicrous. Any engineer knows that the keystone arch is irreducibly complex—it could not stand if any of the arch component blocks are removed. In addition, it could not stand until all of the arch component blocks are in place. But, the engineer also knows that the arch was designed by an intelligent person and that intelligence was necessary for the manufacture of the component parts and the construction of the arch. A keystone arch cannot come into being by itself, which would be a requirement if the analogy is to be valid. The evolutionary explanation for the existence of unknown prior evolutionary processes is indeed magic.

Finally, it would *not* be an honor to be listed in *The Evolution Dialogues* as one of the denominations that "have not found evolution in conflict with their teachings" (p. 169). I will repeat the list again here, but I would say that the proper title for this listing should be the "Christian Hall of Shame":

Lutheran World Federation
Episcopal Church USA
Presbyterian Church (USA)
United Church of Christ
United Methodist Church

I pray that these denominations would experience a quick doctrinal reformation for as the Creator said, "He who is not with me is against me, and he who does not gather with me scatters" (Matthew 12:30). He also said, "Woe to the world because of the things that cause people to sin! Such things must come, but woe to the man through whom they come!" (Matthew 18:7).

We have found that the naturalistic worldview is foundationally and comprehensively at odds with the Word of God. Christians need to understand that the foundational Truth and source of their hope for their eternal lives resides in that Book. Those who try to ignore these facts will be left with extreme consequences as found in Jesus' words in Matthew 7:13, "Enter through the narrow gate. For wide is the gate and broad is the road that leads to destruction, and many enter through it. But small is the gate and narrow the road that leads to life and only a few find it."

FURTHER READING

1. Burgess, Stuart, *Hallmarks of Design: Evidence of Purposeful Design and Beauty in Nature*, Day One Publications, 2000.
2. Dembski, William A., *The Design Revolution: Answering the Toughest Questions About Intelligent Design*, InterVarsity Press, 2004.
3. Morris, Henry M., *History of Modern Creationism*, ICR, 1993.
4. Petersen, Dennis R., *Unlocking the Mysteries of Creation*, Creation Resource Publications, 2002.
5. Sarfati, Jonathan, *By Design: Evidence for Natures' Intelligent Designer—the God of the Bible*, Creation Book Publishers, 2008.

ADVANCING BEYOND DIALOGUE

ANGELA'S STORY—EPILOGUE

ANGELA IS NOW fully indoctrinated into the evolutionary philosophy. She believes she is still a Christian because her university secular environment has modified her understanding of what a Christian believes or can believe. Her biology professor and her religious advisor have helped her move her faith to the point where it is acceptable to believe in a God who is basically unknown and very far away. There is no real need for God's Word since those who are educated in this naturalistic philosophy have accepted a new method for determining truth.

Geologic Formations in John Day area

The Christian religion has been relegated to that part of the human experience where emotion is the only instigator and operator of a person's spiritual life.

Angela now has no problem believing that Oligocene fossil beds contain fossils that are 24 to 34 million years old. She wants to go to a fossil dig so "she can see a creature lying where it fell so long ago, millions of years before any human walked on the earth."[66] People can and do believe anything and that includes believing that they alone can determine who God is. Angela's so-called religious advisor talks about getting out in nature by saying, "It is mysterious territory. It's one of those places where the presence of God is almost palpable."[67]

Yes, for most evolutionists there would be no expectation that God would be perceivable or touchable. For them either God does not exist, one cannot know if He exists, or His existence is irrelevant to a person's daily life. But this vision of God is not my vision of God, nor is it the triune God of the Bible. James wrote on the concept of God's closeness saying, "Submit yourselves, then, to God. Resist the devil, and he will flee from you. Come near to God and he will come near to you" (James 4:7-8a). In Philippians 4:4-5 we read, "Rejoice in the Lord always. I will say it again: Rejoice! Let your gentleness be evident to all. The Lord is near." In Ephesians 2:13 Paul says, "But now in Christ Jesus you who once were far away have been brought near through the blood of Christ."

Even most infants in the faith are familiar with Christ's Great Commission. Here Jesus directed all Christians that they are to go and make disciples of all nations and teach them to obey everything that He commanded be done. He then said, "And surely I am with you always, to the very end of the age" (Matthew 28:20). These are the marching orders for the Christian and are not optional. It is my observation that few Christians who have accepted evolution would ever speak about the Jesus Christ of the Bible in their own home let alone throughout the nations. This is what happens when evolution and millions of years are stirred into the Christian faith.

I wish that it would be possible for me to speak to every reader of *The Evolution Dialogues* so that I could warn them that the God that the writers would have Christians worship is outside of the creation, is unknowable, is impersonal, and is impotent. It is anything but the true God that has been revealed in the Bible and in the creation.

The true God has indeed been intimately involved in His creation from the very beginning. Our Lord Jesus Christ explains, "I was there when he set the heavens in place, when he marked out the horizon on the face of the deep, when he established the clouds above and he fixed securely the fountains of the deep, when he gave the sea its boundary so the waters would not overstep his command, and when he marked out the foundations of the earth" (Proverbs 8:27-29).

He also provides us with an understanding of the options available saying, "For whoever finds me finds life and receives favor from the LORD. But whoever fails to find me harms himself; all who hate me love death" (Proverbs 8:35-36).

ADVANCING BEYOND DIALOGUE

There are just two topics that I will touch on in this epilogue. One is the accusation that biblical creationists and other Darwin doubters are less than truthful, ignoring the historical interaction of scientific and Christian traditions, and are so selective in their use of reason as to distort its results.[68] The other is to examine the benefits of Darwinism to society—if there are any.

When the authors make statements about the integrity of people such as myself that are so accusingly derogatory (saying we are less than truthful) it does not speak well of the humility that they ought to have when interpreting the thoughts of others. In our American society today there are many topics about which people disagree. Yet the evolution vs. creation controversy is a topic where there is an official position that has been dictated by those in control of academia, the media, and the courts. This is not a good situation for the liberty of the citizens of this nation. The whole controversy is over worldview and has nothing to do with science in the true sense of the word. Americans will be worse off each time this type of tyranny is allowed to take hold. It should be apparent that Biblical Christians have no place in their faith for evolution and millions of years, but others who are not believers should see that a successful eradication of the creationist view can only result in steps to gag others whose beliefs do not match up to the thinking and agenda of the leftist elite.

I hope I have made it clear in *The Creation Dialogues* that the AAAS and others like them have no real interest in dialogue concerning this debate. The presuppositions of their faith do not allow for dialogue. When they say they are going to "advance beyond dialogue," they mean that they will continue to repeat the same old arguments only with a louder voice with the expectation that they will eventually drown out any opposing views whether Christian or otherwise.

Today we have a terrible situation where academics who dare question Darwinism are very likely to be penalized for it. I know that many people believe that academia is the place where all viable ideas are accepted, but this is a myth. Those who ignore what is going on in education today have their heads in the sand, and the long-term result will be detrimental for everyone. Diversity has evolved to the point where it often means perversity, and if perversity becomes a standard for a society its collapse cannot be far behind. I suggest that anyone who doubts that this is indeed the situation concerning Darwin doubters should read Jerry Bergman's book *Slaughter of the Dissidents*.[69]

Now let me discuss the issue of the benefits of evolutionary indoctrination to society. As an engineer I know that there is no field of applied science where evolutionary theories have provided any societal benefit. There are no inventions, machines, processes, or discoveries that engineers use in their careers that were made on the basis of macro-evolutionary theories. For example, one of the great "scientific" accomplishments of mankind was the landing of a man on the moon. That was not really a scientific success, but rather was an engineering triumph. Most of the science that allowed the actual delivery and return of the human payload was Newtonian physics. That engineering field of study (orbital mechanics) along with advances in miniaturization and computers were the most important technological engines for the achievement. The only way that evolution entered into the effort is that some of the impetus and justification for spending the huge sums of money for the endeavor came from those who believe space travel might allow for the discovery of life elsewhere in the universe. This would be life that, of course, mysteriously evolved in another place far, far away.

The only reason scientists must accept methodological naturalism as the driving faith basis for their working lives is because if they do not they will be penalized or driven out of the profession. Even biology and medical professors can teach for decades without mentioning evolution.[70] The reason they can do this is that evolution theory adds nothing

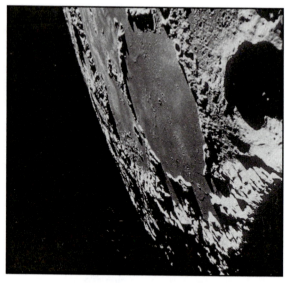

Craters on the Moon

to the ability of physicians, surgeons, and biology researchers to do what they have been trained to do. The only exception to that is that those who are by definition "evolutionary" scientists (the priests of the faith) must teach and write about evolution.

Finally, I close with this warning. Jesus said, "And if anyone causes one of these little ones who believes in me to sin, it would be better for him to be thrown into the sea with a large millstone tied around his neck" (Mark 9:42).

ENDNOTES

1. Dobzhansky, Theodosius, "Evolutionary and Population Genetics," *Science*, vol. 142 (November 29, 1963), pp. 1131-1135.
2. Dobzhansky, Theodosius, "Changing Man," *Science*, vol. 155, no. 3761 (January 27, 1967), pp. 409-415.
3. Kleiss, Richard L. and Christina E., *A Closer Look at the Evidence*, 2003. January 23.
4. Morris, Henry M., *Men of Science Men of God*, 1988, p. 27.
5. Morris, Henry M., *The Defender's Study Bible*, 1995, Appendix 5.
6. Darwin, Charles, *The Origin of Species*, 1859, p. 152.
7. Dawkins, Richard, *The Blind Watchmaker*, 1996, p. 1.
8. *Ibid*, p. 21.
9. Anonymous, "Hoyle on Evolution," *Nature*, vol. 294 (November 12, 1981), p. 105.
10. Jackson, Wayne, *The Human Body: Accident or Design?* 1993, pp. 56-58. (In Kleiss, Richard and Tina, *A Closer Look at the Evidence*, 2003.)
11. Templeton, Charles, *Farewell to God*, McClelland & Stewart, 1996, pp. 198-199.
12. Gould, Stephen Jay, "Evolution's Erratic Pace," *Natural History*, vol. 86 (May 1977), p. 14.
13. Brown, Walt, *In the Beginning*, Seventh Edition, CSC, 2001, p. 6.
14. Dobzhansky, Theodosius, *Evolution, Genetics, and Man*, John Wiley & Sons, 1955, p. 105.
15. Dodson, Peter, *The Horned Dinosaurs*, Princeton University Press, 1996, p. 5.
16. http://www.amnh.org/education/teachersguides/dinosaurs/usingcladistics.html, accessed 3-28-07.

17. Morris, John, "The Real Nature of the Fossil Record," *Acts and Facts*, February 2010, p. 14.

18. For a current evaluation of the true facts surrounding this story see Bergman, Jerry, "The Huxley-Wilberforce Debate Myth," *Creation Research Society Quarterly*, vol. 46 (3) Winter 2010, p. 177.

19. http://themonkeytrial.com. Accessed 2-20-10.

20. http://www.gradesaver.com/inherit-the-wind/study-guide/about/. Accessed 2-20-10.

21. Bergman, Jerry and Howe, George, *Vestigial Organs Are Fully Functional*, CRS, 1990.

22. Junker, Reinhard, *Is Man Descended from Adam?* 1988, p. 26.

23. Vere, Francis, *Lessons of Piltdown*, The Evolution Protest Movement, 1959, p. 2.

24. Bozarth, G. Richard, "The Meaning of Evolution," *American Atheist* (February 1978), p. 30.

25. *Webster's New World Compact School and Office Dictionary*, MacMillan, 1995.

26. Morris, Henry M. and Parker, Gary E., *What is Creation Science?* Mater Books, 1987, p. 9.

27. Morris, Henry, *That Their Words May be Used Against Them*, Master Books, 1997.

28. Broad, William and Wade, Nicholas, *Betrayers of the Truth*, Simon and Schuster, 1982, p. 141.

29. *Ibid.*

30. Patterson, John, "Do Scientists and Educators Discriminate Unfairly against Creationists?" *Journal of the National Center for Science Education* (Fall 1984), p. 19.

31. Bergman, Jerry, *Slaughter of the Dissidents*, Leafcutter Press, 2008.

32. Ruse, Michael, "How Evolution Became a Religion," *National Post* (Ontario, Canada), May, 2000, sec. B., p. 3.

33. Morris, Henry, *What Is Creation Science?* Master Books, 1987, p. 189.

34. Ashcroft, Chris, "James Ossuary Withstands Accusations," *Creation*, 32(1) January-March 2010, p. 43.

35. *Webster's New World Compact School and Office Dictionary*, MacMillan, 1994.

36. DeYoung, Don, *Thousands ... Not Billions*, Master Books, 2005, pp. 158-170.

37. In a letter dated 23 April 1984 to David C.C. Watson, Hebrew Professor James Barr at the University of Oxford as transcribed by Walt Brown in his book, *In the Beginning*, p. 281.

38. Morris, Henry, *The Bible and Modern Science*, Moody Press, 1956, p. 95.

39. McDowell, Josh, *The New Evidence That Demands a Verdict*, Thomas Nelson, 1994, p. 120.

40. Kleiss, Richard L. and Kleiss, Christina E., *A Closer Look at the Evidence*, Search for the Truth Publications, 2003, July 12.

41. Wald, George, "The Origin of Life," in *The Physics and Chemistry of Life*, Simon and Schuster, 1955, p. 270.

42. Dose, Professor Dr. Klaus, "The Origin of Life; More Questions than Answers," *Interdisciplinary Science Reviews*, vol. 13, no, 4 (1988), p. 348.

43. McGinnis, Helen J., *Carnegie's Dinosaurs*, Carnegie Institute, 1982, p. 69.

44. Weston, William, "La Brea Tar Pits: A Critique of Animal Entrapment Theories," *Creation Research Society Quarterly*, vol. 39, no. 2 (December 2002).

45. Weston, William, "La Brea Tar Pits: An Introductory History (1769-1969)," *Creation Research Society Quarterly*, vol. 38, no. 4 (March) 2002).

46. *Rancho La Brea, Death Trap and Treasure Trove*, Los Angeles Country Museum of Natural History Foundation, 2002, p. 15.

47. Weston, William, "La Brea Tar Pits: Evidence of a Catastrophic Flood," *Creation Research Society Quarterly*, vol. 40, no. 1 (June 2003).

48. Morris, John D., *The Young Earth*, Master Books, 1994, p. 70.

49. Lockley, Martin, *Dinosaur Tracks and Other Fossil Footprints of the Western United States*, Columbia University Press, 1995, p. 18.

50. *Ibid*, p. 23.

51. "Fossil Questions and Answers," John Day Fossil Beds National Monument-Painted Hills Unit, August, 2005.

52. From an interpretive highway sign at a rest stop along Route 94 in Eastern Montana.

53. http://www.utah.com/playgrounds/cleveland_lloyd.htm. Accessed 10-17-08.

54. Available from the website www.creationengineeringconcepts.org.

55. "Geology of Arches an Overview," Canyonlands Natural History Association, Arches National Park, 2009.

56. Barnes, F. A., *Canyon Country Dinosaur Tracks and Trackers*, Canyon Country Publications, 1997, p. 9.

57. West, Linda and McKnight, Clint, *Dinosaur, The Dinosaur National Monument Quarry*, Dinosaur Nature Association, 2001, p. 10.

58. Hoesch, William A. and Austin, Steven A., *Impact #370*, "Dinosaur National Monument: Jurassic Park or Jurassic Jumble?" Institute for Creation Research, April 2004.

59. For example, Grande, Lance, *Paleontology of the Green River Formation with a Review of the Fish Fauna*, Wyoming State Geological Survey, 2nd Edition, 2004.

60. Whitmore, J.H., *Experimental Fish Taphonomy with a Comparison to Fossil Fishes*, Ph.D. Dissertation, Loma Linda University, 2003.

61. Woolley, Daniel A., "Fish Preservation, Fish Coprolites and the Green River Formation," *TJ* 15(1) April 2001.

62. Hedeen, Stanley, *Big Bone Lick*, The University Press of Kentucky, 2008, pp.119-120.

63. *Ibid*, p. 123.

64. *The Evolution Dialogues*, p. 151.

65. Scott, Eugenie, "Monkey Business," *The Sciences* (January/February 1996), p. 25.

66. *The Evolution Dialogues*, p. 175.

67. *Ibid*, p. 176.

68. *Ibid,* p. 179.

69. Bergman, Jerry, *Slaughter of the Dissidents*, Leafcutter Press, 2008.

70. Menton, David, *The Evolution of Darwin—His Science* DVD, Answers in Genesis, 2009.

NAME AND SUBJECT INDEX

SCRIPTURE INDEX

LaVergne, TN USA
15 February 2011
216516LV00001B/1-26/P